EXPOSED

EXPOSED

Success Secrets for Landlords

Lestel Meade

Requests for permission should be directed to lestelegram@gmail.com. www.lestel-meade.com/

Library of Congress Control Number: 2022916927

Paperback ISBN: 979-8-2180079-4-2

Editor: Amy Pattee Colvin www.amycolvinwordsmith.com
Interior Design: Amy Pattee Colvin

GET ACCESS TO THE FORMS YOU NEED

READ ME FIRST

To say thanks for reading my book I would like to provide you with some fantastic resources.

Included with your copy of "Exposed Secrets of Successful Landlords" are a number of helpful forms to start you on your Landlord Journey.

www.LANDLORD-LAB.com/FREE-FORMS

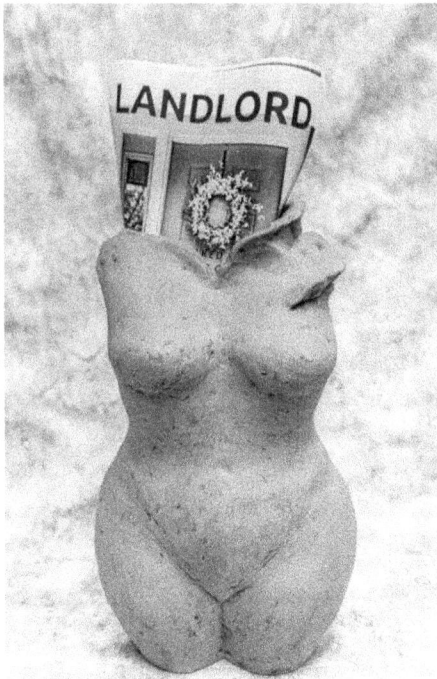

www.LANDLORD-LAB.com

Is your resource for being a successful landlord.

In addition to free rental management forms you can also sign up for a

Free Class

Landlord Lab 101 will provide you with a starting point for becoming a landlord along with vital information and helpful tips.

www.LANDLORD-LAB.com

Landlord Lab
WHERE LANDLORDS COME TO LEARN

Table of Contents

Chapter 1

How It All Began—How I Got Started as a Landlord

When I got started as a landlord, I can say that it was not my idea, and it honestly was not an idea that I was too crazy about. I could say that I was dragged into it. My then-husband and I decided that it was time to buy our first home. We had different ideas as to what we wanted in a home. I wanted a place of our own—not a condo or even a townhome, but a single-family home that was just ours. You know, the great American dream.

Well, my husband had other ideas. He wanted to buy a duplex. He thought it would be great. We would live on one side and rent out the other side to help pay the mortgage. We looked and looked. About two months after we started looking, guess what we bought? We bought a duplex. We lived my husband's dream. Financially it was a great plan. Personally, it was less than ideal. The duplex we purchased was a solid brick beauty built in the mid-1960s. Builders did not believe in or bother with soundproofing back then. Because of the lack of soundproofing, we knew when our tenants were using the bathroom. We also knew when they were brushing their teeth, when they tapped their toothbrush on the side of the sink, and finally, when they turned the water off. We knew what they were watching on TV too. We could hear it all!

Our tenants had not been our selection but the choice of the previous owner, who did not live onsite. Because of Colorado law, we had to honor the tenants' lease. That meant we lived "with" them for the next ten months. They were young, loud and disrespectful. One of the most memorable experiences was when our tenants decided to have a party. The party included lots of people, alcohol, and loud music. They were still going strong at 2:00 a.m. My husband got out of bed at that point and told them to knock it off. They said, "We didn't think we would bother you if we had the party in the garage." We survived the experience and decided to buy another duplex about two years later. Fast forward a bit. My husband and I got a divorce. We split the properties we owned. I got one duplex, and my ex-husband got the other duplex. I was so fed up with being a landlord — remember it was his idea — that I sold my duplex and bought myself a home of my own. I could finally live my dream.

Tax time rolled around that next year, and I could not believe the tax advantages I was missing out on by not having a rental property. I also felt the pain of capital gains taxes. So guess what I did? I bought a condo to use as a rental. I kept that condo for fourteen years before selling it and upgrading to a bigger, newer condo. I have since added an additional home to my rental portfolio.

In addition to my experience as a landlord, I have been a licensed real estate agent in Northern Colorado for nearly twenty-five years. During this time, I have assisted many clients in purchasing their first, second, and all the way to their tenth investment property. I have learned as much from them as they have from me. I have heard their stories, the good, the funny, and the lessons they have learned.

I have sold investment properties to investors who will only buy one-bedroom condos and others who want a varied portfolio of property so that if a particular type of property is not doing well in the market, they are protected. Some investors I have worked with have made sure that the properties they purchased were in various locations to protect them from changes in a particular market. I have learned that a perfect recipe for success in investing in real estate doesn't exist. The most important thing is to take the first step, jump in, and do it!

The purpose of this book is to walk you through the process of becoming a landlord — from the purchase of the property to the day-to-day operation of a rental business. Over the course of the last thirty years as a landlord, I have made mistakes and learned more than I ever thought possible. I want to share what I have learned so that you don't make some of the same mistakes I have.

My goal is for your experience as a landlord to be as smooth as possible. Knowledge can make all of the difference in your success. You may not agree with every aspect of my approach to the rental business, but I will share what has worked for me. This book tells you how to set up your business and reviews the decisions that you will need to make. I go over the advantages and disadvantages, but I do not tell you what you must do, but instead provide you with information so that you can make the decisions for yourself as to how you will run your rental business.

During my years as a landlord, the best advice that I have received came from an older gentleman, Mr. Dean Duncan, who owned an eight-plex right next to our first duplex. I saw an older gentleman working at the eight-plex and struck up a conversation with him. During that conversation, I thought I was talking with the maintenance guy for the owner. However, it soon became clear that I was speaking with the owner himself. I asked him if he had any words of wisdom for a newbie to the rental business. He thought for a while, and he said that he did not have words of wisdom, but he had one word. He paused and looked at me. Waiting for me to ask what that word was. So I asked what that one word of advice would be. He told me the word was patience. If you're like me, you are wondering what patience has to do with being a landlord. So, I asked him. He said that in all that you do as a landlord, remember that word. Let that word be your guiding principle. If you are working on getting your place rented, be patient. If you have a tenant that is a bit of a problem, be patient. That word helped me survive those ten long months with our first tenants. It has been an important word for me to remember throughout all of my years as a landlord and has helped me with my many tenants and business situations. I hope the word becomes an important word for you too. Now that you have been patient reading my story, let's get you started on the path to becoming a landlord.

My function as a writer is not story-telling but truth-telling: to make things plain.

–Laura Riding

Chapter 2

Have You Ever Considered Being a Landlord?

Is becoming a landlord something that you have ever considered? Perhaps the last time you met with your financial planner, she suggested that it might be wise for you to buy an investment property. You may think that the easiest way for you to become a landlord is to turn your current residence into a rental and then move into something that better works for you and your family. But you feel like being a landlord is something you know nothing about. So what do you do? Why should you become a landlord? Let's go over some of the benefits of investing in real estate and answer some of the many questions you may have.

Becoming a landlord is one of the most appealing types of entrepreneurship, but it is not right for everyone. It is important to know the risks and struggles you could face. The advantages of investing in real estate are numerous. As an investor, you can enjoy predictable rental income from your tenants (a cash flow), appreciation on your investment, tax benefits, and the diversification that your financial planner may have been suggesting. With real estate, you can play an active role in your investment. You also have greater control over your investment. You can decide what specific improvements or renovations you would like to make to your investment property to increase the property's value.

Investing in real estate is less risky than investing money in the stock market. Andrew Carnegie was one of the most successful businessmen ever. At its peak, his fortune was worth over $300 Billion (in 2007 dollars). He is attributed with saying that ninety percent of all millionaires become so through owning real estate. He died in 1919. However, real estate is currently on the list of the top-ten creators of billionaires. However, you are looking at just owning a couple of properties and don't realistically imagine yourself a billionaire. Yet, owning rental property is something many ordinary people do. Data released by the United States Census Bureau in 2015 shows that individual owners owned 77.4 percent of rentals. Those are people just like you!

What does all of this mean? It means that people just like you can own real estate and be successful landlords. You can build wealth and appreciate the benefits of owning rental property.

Setting yourself up for success includes many little details. Make a list and start setting up some appointments to meet with professionals who can help you. You will want to talk to a mortgage lender, your real estate agent, and a good attorney. You will want to ask questions like: How much do I need for a down payment? What interest rate will I be charged on an investment property? How will the loan on my investment property be different from the loan on my primary residence? Is this a good location to attract tenants? Will my investment see good appreciation at this location? Is this fixer-upper worth the investment, and why? How much can I charge for rent on this property? Is it better to buy a condo or a single-family home? Arm yourself with information. Research, research, research.

Maintain a business mindset. Your rental property is a business with legal obligations that you must follow. Learn how to manage the property effectively. Create systems for handling maintenance requests. Have a list of professionals you can call, including a handyman, plumber, electrician, real estate agent, attorney and locksmith. Know your rights and understand the rental laws. Have a local attorney draw up your lease—this is essential. Your lease is the most important document for your new rental business. A well-drawn-up lease will protect you and provide you and your tenants with a guide and expectations for both of you!

Armed with professionals to consult when you need information, the basic "how-tos"—including information on the process and a good lease— you, too, can be a successful landlord. We will cover the details and expand on all these concepts, so if you feel overwhelmed, don't worry. We'll work through everything together and review the steps involved in the process so you are comfortable.

In the next chapter, we will review why you should invest in real estate and what the numbers might look like if you take the plunge into becoming a landlord.

Chapter 3

Why Should I Invest in Real Estate?

So you are thinking about investing in real estate. Here is what you should know about the benefits and why real estate is considered a good investment. Several methods for investing in real estate are available. You can purchase property to flip it—in other words, you can purchase a distressed property, fix it up, and resell it for a profit. You can buy a property at a low price and sell it for market value—that would be buying wholesale and selling retail. Or you can invest in real estate for the long term and rent the property. Most real estate investors agree that leasing a property and holding on to the property long-term provides the best outcome and the least risky return.

Buying property as an investment and renting it out is a large undertaking. It can also be very rewarding. Today with all of the information available for new and experienced landlords, being a landlord is easier than ever. Everything from advertising, screening tenants, and management can be done simply and efficiently. Here are some reasons why you should take the plunge and become a landlord.

Advantages

Real estate has high leverage
What does that mean? This means that you can more easily get a real estate loan than other investment options. Imagine going into your bank and

saying that you would like to open up a line of credit for $300,000 so that you could invest in the stocks and bonds while telling them you only had $60,000 for security. The banker would probably smile and usher you out of the bank's door. But envision going into the same bank and telling them that you would like to buy an investment property. You say you have $60,000 for a down payment and would like to borrow $300,000; they would walk you to the mortgage department and start the loan process for you. This different reaction is because the bank sees a real estate investment as much less risky than stocks and bonds. The bank believes that the return on your investment is much more likely to occur, leading to less risk for you and the bank.

Diversification of your assets

Your financial planner may have suggested investing in real estate through buying an investment property. This diversifies your whole portfolio of assets, so your assets are not solely in stocks, bonds and mutual funds. The more spread out your money is, the less likely you will fare poorly everywhere. Stocks may do poorly, but real estate is seeing great appreciation, so you are making money on real estate, even if you are losing money on your investment in stocks.

Appreciation

One of the wonderful things about real estate is that it is an asset that appreciates over time. The longer you own your property, the more that it will be worth. With real estate, your down payment is appreciated in addition to the actual asset. The whole of it is appreciated. This means you are building equity.

Also, with real estate, you can research the market and learn the best location in which to invest, whether your preferred investment is a one-bedroom condo or a single-family home. You can learn trends and make informed decisions about the market, making real estate a less volatile investment compared to other options like stocks and bonds, where reactions to the market can be hard to predict as an investor.

Stable cash flow (income)

The purpose of purchasing a rental property is to rent it out to a tenant. By renting the property, you are earning an income. The income should cover the principal, interest, taxes, insurance on the property, and the HOA if that is applicable. The income should also cover maintenance and upkeep. That income should increase over time and benefit you as you pay down the mortgage and build equity.

Tax benefits

Owning real estate allows for many different kinds of tax deductions. If you have not used an accountant or CPA to do your taxes before, now may be a great time to start. Here are some of the deductions you expect to use now that you own an investment property.

- **Interest:** Landlords can deduct the interest portion of your mortgage payment
- **Depreciation:** The property can be depreciated over its useful life of 27.5 years for residential properties.
- **Repairs:** The costs of repairs are deductible in the year in which they are done. So if you change out the garage door opener, replace the water heater or do other repairs, all are deductible costs.
- **Insurance:** You can deduct the insurance premiums from any insurance policy that has to do with your rental investment.
- **Legal and Professional Services:** You can deduct fees that you pay attorneys, accountants, property management companies and other professionals.

This list does not include all possible deductions but does give you an idea of what tax write-offs you can use. In general, you can deduct the reasonable costs of owning, operating and managing a property. The benefits of using tax deductions help you keep more of your taxable income in your pocket.

Disadvantages

It is not fair to mention all of these benefits without touching on some of the disadvantages. What are the negatives to owning an investment property?

Lack of liquidity

The greatest disadvantage to owning an investment property is that your investment is not liquid. To get your money out of the property, you would have to sell or refinance to pull cash out. Neither of these options will get you cash quickly. Selling could take more than thirty days, and refinancing might take almost as long. Both of these options, selling and refinancing, will cost you money.

Time required

The other disadvantage is the time involved in running your business, including twenty-four-hour availability. You must make sure that you are available if your tenants need you. Water heaters and furnaces usually do not quit working between 8:00 a.m. and 5:00 p.m. You must be ready to deal with the repairs and maintenance of the property. You are responsible for keeping the property in good condition for your tenants.

Financial obligations

As the landlord, you are responsible for the mortgage payment if the property is occupied or vacant. You also need to budget for the unexpected—legal expenses regarding a problem tenant, repairs to the property, or any unforeseen large expense.

Buying a property and renting it is very beneficial; however, it is vital to remember that this is a responsibility. Tenants do not always pay rent on time, things break, and you have to work to find a suitable tenant so that the property is not vacant. The rewards for most people outweigh the disadvantages. You must decide what is right for you. One way to feel the rewards without the hassle may be through hiring a property management company. We will discuss this option later in the book.

Next, let us look at a specific real estate investment scenario. See if you can imagine yourself doing this.

Real estate cannot be lost or stolen, nor can it be carried away. Purchased with common sense, paid for in full, and managed with reasonable care, it is about the safest investment in the world.

–Franklin D. Roosevelt

Chapter 4

Let's Look at the Numbers

We have talked about the advantages and disadvantages of investing in real estate, and you are feeling curious. A curious mind is open to further exploration of an idea. That is a good place to be. If you are like most people, you don't just want to hear that investing in real estate is a good idea; you want to see an example of what this might look like for you. After reviewing this specific example, talk with your preferred lender to see what an investment scenario might look like for you. By exploring with a lender, you can see the specific numbers for your down payment and the amount you would like to spend on a property. For now, let's look at an example of a purchase and see what the numbers look like in this scenario. Is it possible for you to do this?

Here is an example of a successful investment and what you might expect the numbers to look like. In this example, you can find and put under contract a property priced at $340,000. You offer $1,000 more to get your offer accepted and ensure that you go under contract on this property. So the contract price is $341,000. You are putting twenty-five percent down to purchase the property. Your initial investment to purchase is $89,567. That includes your down payment and your loan closing costs. Your loan amount on the property is $255,750. For this example, your monthly PITI (Principal, Interest, Taxes, Insurance) is $1,801.53.

> **A Helpful Hint**! To receive the lowest interest rate on a loan for an investment property, it is best to put twenty-five percent down rather than the standard 20 percent for a conventional loan. Verify this with your local, preferred lender to ensure this will be the case in your situation.

Property details
- Purchase Price: $341,000
- Loan Amount: $255,750
- PITI Payments: $1,801.53
- Initial Investment: $89,567

In this example, we will make some assumptions. One assumption is that the appreciation of the property in the real estate market where it is located is five percent a year. Remember, in our example, you put twenty-five percent down when purchasing the property. We'll also assume the interest rate on your loan is 5.25 percent. Another assumption that we'll make is that during the time that you owned the property, you were charging $1,850 a month in rent. You kept the rental rate the same during the five years you owned the property.

Assumptions
- Appreciation: 5% per year
- Initial investment: 25% down and 5.25% interest rate
- Rent: $1,850 per month
- Selling Costs: 7%

Now let us look at what has happened with your investment after just five years. During this time, you have collected $2,908.20 more in rent than has been paid in mortgage payments (PITI). Based on the five percent appreciation, you will have $199,946.75 in equity, plus the selling costs. This leaves you with a gain of $79,914.91. You add that number to your amount of income over the cost of your mortgage, and you have a net income of $82,832.11.

A return of 92.45 percent return on your investment. How is it possible to have an 18.49 percent return every year? In a word, leverage—otherwise known as using borrowed money to invest. Even though you put twenty-five percent down, you receive one-hundred percent of the appreciation. Because of that, the return is noticeably higher.

Let's look at another example.

If you had bought that same house and paid cash for the property rather than taking out a mortgage, you would have received $84,460 more in rent than expenses since there's no mortgage. That amount plus the appreciation, minus the cost to sell the property, minus the initial investment, has a net gain of $144,207. So 41.80 percent return over five years or 8.36 percent per year. Still not bad, but nowhere near as good as if you had leveraged it. If you consider investing in real estate and thought you would pay cash for the property, you might reconsider and instead purchase more than one property with money down and a mortgage. So your total investment is the same but stretched over more than one property.

Through this example, you can see the amazing financial benefits found by investing in real estate. This example is conservative. Most real estate markets have been seeing much higher appreciation in recent years. Most investors today are able to get lower interest rates than what was used in this example. Even with these conservative numbers, you can see the benefits. It is tough to find another low-risk investment that can give you that high a return. What your involvement looks like with your investment is up to you. That is what this book is about. Let's see how you can be a landlord and enjoy building wealth, but first, we will look at why you would not invest in real estate.

Don't wait to buy real estate. Buy real estate and wait.

–Will Rogers

Chapter 5

Reasons Why You Won't Invest in Real Estate

You have been seriously considering investing in real estate. You have invested time in researching and have weighed the pros and cons and risks and rewards. Time has also been spent talking to people you trust about the idea. But even with all of the support for the concept, you cannot bring yourself to invest in this low-risk investment. Why not?

It is difficult to find people that will tell you investing in real estate is a bad idea. Most see that it is a great way to build wealth. Ninety-four percent of investors who have invested in real estate in the past are planning on investing again. The reasons are there to do it. But I often hear from people who say, "I just can not do it." What are the common reasons people do not take the plunge and invest?

Lack of capital

Many people will say that they just can not save the twenty to twenty-five percent that it takes to put down on a property. The traditional way of investing in real estate does take time and requires that you save money and prepare for the investment. Other ways to invest in real estate are available, including the "no money down" infomercials seen on late-night TV. The methods suggested in these programs are a bit riskier than the typical ways to invest but might work. If you are looking for a shortcut, you might consider turning your current property into your investment property and buying a different primary residence with only five percent down. There are other ways to come up with that down payment, but we are talking about why you won't do this.

Lack of time

You may feel that you do not have the time to find a property to purchase. What do you do with your free time? I know the kids have sports. You have a hobby that means a lot to you that you spend your time doing. Do either of these ways that you spend your time make you money? Real estate agents make it their job to find you the property that will work as an investment property for you. If you feel like the lack of time keeps you from investing, make sure that you are looking at the turnkey properties that are in great condition and may already have a tenant in them. This saves you time finding a tenant and doing work on the property. You do not need too many property options to evaluate—too many options can be overwhelming. At the end of the day, you need one property that has a positive cash flow when you do the math. That positive cash flow does not need to be hundreds of dollars a month. It needs to meet the financial obligations of principal, interest, taxes, and insurance on the property and the HOA dues, if applicable. It is nice to have a couple of hundred dollars a month so that you can build savings for the maintenance issues when they arise.

If you are afraid of the lack of time to manage the property after you own it, you can spend the money and have a property management company manage it for you. Remember to consider the cost involved in your figures to ensure that you still will have a positive cash flow.

Lack of confidence

Risk is a scary thing. It is not for those faint of heart. Risk is what keeps many investors from leaping into real estate. The fear of risk can paralyze and overwhelm you, leading you to doubt yourself and be uncertain when making well-informed decisions. This is where you lean on your trusted advisors and look to them to give you the push of encouragement to jump in and do it. Those trusted advisors can help you evaluate the specific risk.

Lack of confidence can also come from a lack of knowledge. To deal with your lack of confidence, you will need to spend time researching and educating yourself so that you know when you see a good deal and can move forward. We were not born with the knowledge of real estate investing. You may not know anyone who is an investor. If this is the case, join an investment group and learn from those that have success doing what you desire to do, even if the group is on social media. Take a class and read about it. Knowledge can give you confidence.

Are you going to let these reasons stop you from investing in real estate? You are capable! You can do it! But there are questions you will need to answer before you jump in. What do you want to own? The next chapter will examine the options that are available to you.

Landlords grow rich in their sleep without working, risking, or economizing.

–John Stuart Mill

Chapter 6

What Should I Purchase?

When becoming a landlord, the first step is to acquire a property to rent. You might be in a situation where you decide to use your current property as a rental and purchase something else that better suits your current needs. But if you are in the market to buy, how do you decide what to buy? Many choices are available. Do you buy a condo/townhome, a single-family home, or perhaps a duplex like I did? What are the advantages and disadvantages of each type of property?

One of the first things to consider is what type of tenant you would like to have in your rental. The type of rental you purchase affects the type of tenant you have. For example, if you purchase a one-bedroom condo, you will have a limited number of people that will live in your rental. A single-family home that has four bedrooms will attract another type of tenant. If you purchase a condo near the University, you will more likely have students as your tenants. Know that as a landlord, you cannot discriminate against the protected classes, which will be covered in greater detail later. Still, your selection of a rental will naturally attract certain types of tenants.

A Helpful Hint! Did you know if you purchase a property that tenants currently occupy, you are required by law, as the new owner of the property, to honor the lease terms currently in place?

Condo/Townhome

A condo/townhome provides you with a property where you typically are concerned solely with interior maintenance. Not worrying about the exterior may offer you some peace of mind. You pay a monthly fee to the HOA to cover the exterior maintenance. Your unit is typically painted for you, the lawn is mowed, snow is removed, and there are no lawn sprinklers to worry about. The dues might even cover the roof. In addition to the exterior maintenance being covered, the HOA dues may cover trash, water, and sewer. This can mean much easier ownership for you and less maintenance overall for you as the landlord. If you consider purchasing a condo/townhome, make sure you understand exactly what the HOA dues cover. I have listed many things that could be covered, but make sure you know the specifics for any property you are considering.

The HOA may keep watch on your tenant and their activities too. You may receive notification that your tenant has too many vehicles parked at the property. You may hear that the neighbor has voiced a noise complaint regarding your tenant. You may know more about what is going on at your rental than you really want to know because of the HOA and the community management company. This may be something that you consider to be an advantage.

With the HOA maintaining the outside, you only have to worry about the unit's interior. If the tenant causes significant damage, you may only need to repaint or replace the carpet or other flooring before you are ready to rent the property to another tenant. The tenant has less responsibility. A tenant can live carefree and only worry about keeping the inside of the unit presentable. Another advantage to purchasing a condo/townhome is affordability. Condos/townhomes in most real estate markets are not as expensive as single-family homes, which means that a condo/townhome can be a great inexpensive start to your real estate rental business.

Another benefit to a condo/townhome is that the size of the unit is typically smaller. Smaller square footage and number of bedrooms and baths means that you will naturally be renting the unit to fewer people. That can mean less wear and tear, fewer people, and minimized headaches for you, the landlord.

A possible disadvantage to owning a condo/townhome as a rental is that you may not see quite the same level of appreciation as you would with owning a single-family home as a rental. Check with your real estate agent to know what the market is like where you are considering investing. Another disadvantage is that when factoring in regular HOA dues, you may not have a positive cash flow on the property. This may rule out properties that would otherwise make a great rental.

HOA dues on a condo/townhome regularly increase. Check and compare the HOA dues of the different complexes you are considering. The dues can vary significantly between the complexes. Amenities that are offered can vary between complexes too. The amenities offered in a condo/townhome project can provide a quality lifestyle to a prospective tenant. They are not just renting a place to live; they have desirable things available to them to do. Amenities like a pool, tennis courts, workout facilities, and lake surface rights may be offered. The more amenities available for the prospective tenant to use, the more attractive your rental may be and the more a prospective tenant may be willing to pay in rent.

Single-family home

There are several advantages to purchasing a single-family home as an investment property. The first advantage is having more properties to choose from. This can be a major asset in your search. You are not only able to select the neighborhood but the house with just the right features that will help you get the highest rent. Another advantage of purchasing a single-family home is buying a property that typically has more space than a condo/townhome. It is likely, in many markets, that you will see greater appreciation in a single-family home over a condo/townhome. This means that you may get a higher return on your investment over time. The more affordable the property you are purchasing, the greater the possibility of significant appreciation. Demand is greater at the lower end of the market, which drives the appreciation. If there is a shortage of affordable homes in the lower price range, this will also drive appreciation up.

Disadvantages to using a single-family home as investment property are that both the interior of the home and the exterior need to be maintained by either the tenant or you, the landlord. These maintenance responsibilities include lawn care in the summer, snow removal in the winter, the roof, and exterior paint. As the landlord, you can require the tenants to mow and maintain the lawn and shovel the snow, but this may be a responsibility that the tenant does not want. Opportunities for property damage also increase with single-family homes, and not just the inside. A single-family home is typically more expensive to purchase and requires a higher down payment.

Other real estate options for investment are worth considering, like an apartment building or a duplex. These options are called multi-family. What you choose as an investment, in the end, comes down to your personal preference and how much money you have to work with. Your selection can depend on how involved you would like to be as a landlord.

A Helpful Hint! Once you have decided what you would like to purchase, it is time to sit down with a real estate agent and specifically tell them what you are interested in purchasing. I am suggesting a sit-down, across-the-desk meeting. During that meeting, lay out specifically what you want and have them begin your search.

One option for a rental is turning the property you already own into a rental and purchasing something different that you would prefer to live in. Is this option right for you? We will explore this question in the next chapter.

Chapter 7

Should I Turn My Current Home into Rental?

One way to become a landlord is to turn your current home into a rental and move yourself to a home that you find more pleasing. It seems easy. You do not need to sell your home. The only thing required is moving out and renting it to someone. But, what should be considered before committing to doing this?

If you plan to keep your current home and use it as a rental, it is essential to determine if you will qualify for another mortgage. Will your lender use the possible income from the rental to help you qualify? Do you need to have a signed lease to use that rental income?

How long have you lived in your current home? Mortgages for owner-occupants require that you live in the home and use it as your primary residence for at least twelve months. One of the perks offered to owner-occupants is a lower interest rate on their mortgage. Moving out early and turning the property into a rental could be considered mortgage fraud. The lender could recall the loan, and if you could not pay the loan off in full, the lender could begin foreclosure. Make sure that you have met the lender's requirements for owner occupancy.

Another consideration is whether you have refinanced in the last twelve months. You could find yourself in a similar mortgage fraud situation if you have refinanced recently. If you have lived in the property for more than twelve months and have not refinanced in the last twelve months, then it could be possible for you to use your home as a rental.

Also, depending on how long you have lived in your current home and whether you have refinanced for cash out, you may have significant equity. This could mean a mortgage payment well below the rental amount you can charge for the property. The next question that you need to ask is if it is possible to rent your home for enough to cover the mortgage payment and expenses? It is ideal to have a positive cash flow after expenses have been met. If your figures show that you would be lucky enough to have that "extra" cash left over after expenses, remember that "extra" should be put away for maintenance and repairs.

Check with the HOA — if your home is in an area governed by an HOA — to make sure that they allow rentals. Some HOA's have restrictions regarding using a property as a rental; they may restrict the total number of rentals or the location of rentals within the neighborhood. They also may restrict the lease term, not allowing shorter-term rentals. Remember that your tenants will be required to follow the rules and regulations of the HOA as well.

By turning your current home into a rental, you experiment with being a landlord. If you do not like the experience or you feel it just does not work for you, you can turn around and sell the home. If you have lived in the home for two of the last five years, you can sell the home without paying capital gains if your gain is less than $250,000 for a single person and $500,000 for a married couple. Make sure that these numbers have not changed and that you are up to date on the rules about capital gains.

No one knows your home better than you. Because you are familiar with the home and have lived there, you know the home's quirks, the expenses, and what to expect. You know the maintenance schedule, age of appliances, and how much use they have had. You will have fewer surprises because you know the property. You can also prepare the home to use as a rental while you live there, painting and making repairs all before you move. You also know the neighbors, and they may be willing to help you keep an eye on the property and alert you to what is happening.

If you are staying in the area, managing one single-family home nearby could be the easiest rental property you could have, allowing you to test being a landlord to see if it is right for you.

A Helpful Hint! Remember that if you are planning on turning your home into a rental, you will need to change the insurance for the property. Call your insurance agent before your tenant moves in.

Don't look for the needle in the haystack. Just buy the haystack.

–Jack Bogle

Chapter 8

Should I Buy a Property for My College Student?

Another way to become a landlord is to purchase a home/townhome/condo for your college student to live in throughout college. First, of course, you have to have a college-age child. If you have a college-age child, making this rental purchase is pretty simple. You purchase the property that is acceptable to you and your child. Your child selects roommates. A lease is signed by the roommates, and you become the landlord. This could be an easy way to get your start. I have helped many parents of college students through the purchase of a property and setting them up as a landlord to their children and tenants/roommates.

How might this situation work? Even if the school does not require it, I would recommend that your student stays in the dorm for their first year of college. This allows them to get adjusted to college life, meet people, and demonstrate that they can handle school and all that goes with it. Then just before the beginning of their second year of school, you purchase a property for them to live in. At this point, your student will know other students that they like and would get along with as roommates. The roommates sign the lease and help pay the mortgage. This can be a great situation for all involved. So, what are the advantages and disadvantages of this idea?

Advantages
1. You will have more control over your child's living situation. When my college-age son was looking for affordable living situations, I went along for some of the viewings and was appalled at what was being

charged for disgusting properties that I certainly did not want my child living in.

2. You offer an affordable living situation for your student. Ideally, having your child living with roommates in a property you have purchased will be less expensive than your child renting somewhere else. This is certainly the goal. As the buyer for the property that your student will be living in, you have some control over the price of the purchased property and, therefore, could ensure that the numbers work in order to save money.

3. By purchasing a property for your student to live in for sophomore through senior year of college, you will know your child's living situation each year, and you may avoid the hassles of moving at the end of each school year.

4. You will know the tenants, or at least your student will know the tenants. No one ever knows someone until you live with them, but you at least have some idea.

5. Owning a property with your student living in it can teach some responsibility or at least provide the opportunity to have your child manage tenant problems and maintenance of the property. Your student could be responsible for regularly changing the furnace filter and other routine maintenance. You could also let the tenants know that they are to inform your student of things that break. Your student would then notify you, and you would work with them to resolve the issue. This situation may not work for all students and parents. You may need to bypass your student and have the tenants contact you directly. But this situation can lend itself to teachable moments. You know best what your student can and may not be able to handle and what you are comfortable with.

A Helpful Hint! When signing a lease with students, it is crucial to sign one-year leases. This may be different than what they are accustomed to, but certainly in your best interest.

Disadvantages

1. There may be some awkwardness in being a landlord to your child's friends.

2. The situation may require more involvement on your part, dealing with personality issues or situations between the roommates. For example, one of the students drops out of school or just cannot handle the living

situation that was so appealing when they signed the lease and must move. This may require time to find tenants in the middle of the school year.

3. Maintenance can be a bit of an issue. Students have a tendency not to report issues until they are big problems. Also, you probably do not live locally and have to manage maintenance from a distance. Students also may not take care of things like an older tenant might.

4. At the end of the lease period, issues may arise about returning the security deposit. If common areas are damaged, who is responsible for the damage? It is easy if the student is renting a room. Any damage in their room they are responsible for. But they also use the living area, the kitchen and the laundry. What do you do with damage found in those areas?

5. Many of the disadvantages can be removed by using a property management company. Make sure the numbers work to do this. Having a student living in a property that you own can make the college living experience much simpler. You have the advantage of having some control over the living situation and cost. You also have some control over the typical problems with roommates and drama that students can have when living with each other.

6. In renting to students, you may constantly have changes in who is living in the house. This can be even with a lease that lasts a year. Students may break the lease because they drop out of school or find issues with their living situation. Some do not take the lease agreement that they signed seriously. They are responsible until the room can be rented to someone else. This is my policy. You will have to decide how you would like to deal with the breaking of the lease. If you are only renting a room, it can be difficult sometimes to find a new roommate that will be approved by all that are living in the house.

Another consideration to examine while evaluating is the predicted appreciation for the community where you would be purchasing the property. All of this information can help you decide whether it makes good financial sense to purchase a property for your college student and roommates.

Connect with a real estate agent in the community where your student will reside to learn more about the real estate market.

Before you start trying to work out which direction the property market is headed, you should be aware that there are markets within markets.

–Paul Clitheroe

Chapter 9

Process of Buying an Investment Property

Once you are ready to move forward on purchasing an investment property and you are clear on the type of property that interests you, the next step is to get pre-approved for a loan. Now is the time to get recommendations from people you know for a great loan officer and lending institution. It is important to work with a loan officer with experience and creativity to help you with the financing of this purchase.

The process of purchasing an investment property can be a bit different from purchasing a primary residence. However, some things are the same. You may choose to do a thirty-year, fifteen-year, or even a ten-year mortgage. You also can typically close the transaction in approximately thirty days. So what is different? When purchasing an investment property, twenty percent down is required. If you can put twenty-five percent down, you will be able to get a lower interest rate on the loan. The down payment cannot be gift funds but can come from savings, stocks, bonds, or a home equity line of credit (HELOC) on your primary residence. You can also refinance an existing property to obtain the down payment. Unfortunately, because of the greater risk of defaulting on an investment property loan, the interest rate for that loan will be higher. When you apply for a loan on an investment property, you will be able to use seventy-five percent of the expected rent to qualify.

You have provided the lender with all required documentation and completed the loan application. Now, wait to hear those words, "You are pre-approved," before you start looking at properties. Ensure that the loan officer is prepared to issue a pre-approval letter if you find the perfect property. Sometimes the loan officer will tell you that you are pre-qualified. Have the loan officer take the extra time to guarantee that they are in a position to issue the pre-approval letter. This might mean that the loan application process is a bit more detailed and might take a bit longer. When the pre-approval process is complete, you can write an offer on a property. Your offer has a greater chance of being accepted by a seller when the loan officer can provide the pre-approval letter to accompany the offer.

> **A Helpful Hint!** When applying for a mortgage loan, it is important to keep the following in mind. Whether this is your mortgage for your first investment property, a home equity line of credit (HELOC) on your primary residence, or a refinance, the following information can make the difference between successfully getting a loan and having your loan denied. This time can be stressful, and it may be easy to forget the cans and can-nots of this loan process.

Dos and don'ts of the application process

- Don't deposit cash into your bank accounts. Lenders need to source your money, and cash is not really traceable. Small, explainable deposits are fine, but getting a gift of $10,000 in cash is not. Discuss the proper way to track your assets with your loan officer.
- Don't make any large purchases like a new car or a bunch of new furniture. New debt could include new monthly obligations. New obligations create new qualifications. People with new debt have higher debt ratios, making for riskier loans. This can mean that some qualified borrowers no longer qualify.
- Don't co-sign on other loans for anyone. When you co-sign, you are obligated. With that obligation comes higher debt ratios as well. Even if you swear you won't be making payments, the lender will be counting the payment against you.
- Don't change bank accounts. Remember, lenders need to source and track assets. That task is significantly easier when there is a consistency of accounts. Frankly, before you even transfer money between accounts, talk to your loan officer.
- Don't apply for new credit. It doesn't matter whether it's a new credit card or a new car; when you have your credit report run by organizations in multiple financial channels—mortgage credit card, auto, and so on—your FICO score will be affected. Lower credit scores

can determine your interest rate and your eligibility for approval of the loan.

- Don't close any credit accounts. Many clients have erroneously believed that having less available credit makes them less risky and more approvable for a mortgage. *Wrong.* A major component of your score is your length and depth of credit history—as opposed to just your payment history—and your total usage of credit as a percentage of available credit. Closing accounts hurts both those determinants of your score. The best advice is to fully disclose and discuss your plans with your loan officer before doing anything financial. Any blip in income, assets, or credit should be reviewed and executed in a way to keep your application in the most positive light.

The next step in this process is to connect with a great real estate agent. Find one that is an expert in the local market rather than a generalist about many areas. It is ideal if they own investment properties themselves. You will need an agent that can help you evaluate the options available to you to determine which of those is likely to be a profitable rental. A good agent can also let you know the likely rent on a property and how common vacancies are in your area. It will be important to crunch the numbers. Remember that this business decision makes it different from the emotional decision you perhaps made when purchasing your primary home.

During your search for an investment property, you may view properties that have tenants occupying them. These properties would provide you with a ready-made landlord-tenant situation. During your showing, in addition to seeing the overall condition of the property, you can also view how the tenants take care of the property. This might be a starting place for you. In Colorado, you are required to honor the lease that is in place; in other words, the lease survives the sale of the property. Check to see what the regulation is in your state.

It is important to evaluate the situation and make sure that the property lease is not undervalued and that the numbers still work. With a tenant in place for the length of the lease, these properties do not work for everyone. For example, a first-time home buyer looking at purchasing a personal residence must occupy the property within fifty-nine days of the closing. In addition, the tenants living in the property may be less than cooperative with the selling process. Tenants can make showings difficult by not making the property look its best for showings, not allowing showings when the showing is requested and then being present for the showings. All of this can make prospective buyers uncomfortable. This can also make a longer marketing time for the property. Because of this, you may be able to purchase a property with a tenant in place for slightly below market value. Properties like this are certainly something that you will want to consider.

So you have found the place that you think will work as your rental. You have checked, and the numbers work. You are ready to have your agent write up the offer.. Make sure that you know the market. Is it possible to offer less than asking and still have a chance of buying the property? What percentage of the asking price are homes selling for? Ask these questions of your agent before submitting an offer.

Make sure that you know what is important to the seller so that, if possible, you can include that in your offer to make it as attractive as possible. This can be learned by a quick phone call by your agent to the sellers' agent. Money isn't the only aspect of a contract. The timing of dates in the contract, possession of the property, and how much money you can put down on the property are all part of the equation. All of these may matter to the seller. Once your offer is submitted to the seller, the seller has three options. They can accept the offer as it was written, reject the offer, or counter the offer, changing things in the contract that the seller does not find acceptable. Once the offer has been negotiated and accepted, the under-contract process begins, and you'll find much to do, as the buyer, during this period. Make sure that you are in regular communication with your lender and your real estate agent to ensure that you are taking care of the necessary items you are responsible for.

A Helpful Hint! Verify, when you have your lease prepared for you, that you do not have a requirement for twenty-four hours' notice for you to gain access to the property. If you are shown tenant-occupied properties, you may not be allowed to view a property without twenty-four-hour notice, per the tenants' lease. In my opinion, twenty-four-hours' notice is too much notice and a hassle for the landlord and prospective buyers if you choose to sell your property. Don't make that same mistake.

Step by step process of buying an investment property
1. Decide what type of property you want to buy.
2. Get pre-approved for a loan.
3. Set a budget.
4. Connect with a great real estate agent.
5. View possible properties.

6. Write a contract.
7. The contract is negotiated and accepted by the seller.
8. Title work is ordered and should be reviewed on the property.
9. Inspection is completed by a home inspector.
10. The condition of the property is negotiated.
11. You obtain insurance on the property.
12. The property is appraised.
13. Final figures for closing are provided.
14. Do a final walkthrough of the property.
15. It's closing day, and you close on the property and begin your journey as a landlord.

As a buyer, one of the first steps in the under-contract process is to order the inspection. Check with your agent for a referral to a reputable inspector. Please do not do the inspection yourself. An inspector does this for a living and knows what to look for and what to check in the home to ensure that everything is working correctly. Typically an inspector will spend two to three hours at the property, inspecting everything from the roof to the furnace, appliances, light fixtures, and everything in between. Make sure that you attend the inspection, or at least find out when the inspector will be wrapping up and show up at the end so that the inspector can show you their concerns. This is also a good time to have the inspector show you the main water shut-off location and how to change the furnace filter—all valuable information to know.

Once the inspection has been completed, you should receive a report. Review the report and then decide what to request that the seller repair or replace. Ask for guidance from your real estate agent as to what is customary to request given the current market. Know that the inspector will not find everything, no matter how wonderfully thorough they are. You may have to spend some money after closing on repairs. This is not because the inspector did not do a good job inspecting the property; it just happens. Spending two to three hours in the property is not the same as the knowledge gained by living in a property or owning a property.

During the process of negotiating the inspection, you should have received title work on the property. Review the title work, and ask your real estate agent questions regarding things you do not understand. Title work can be an interesting history lesson. You may learn that the land that your property sits on was once owned by a railroad. You also may learn that there are mineral rights with the property. If there are mineral rights, make sure they are included and transferred at closing. To have the rights included may require additional paperwork. Mineral rights could mean a small additional income on your property.

The next step in the under-contract process is the appraisal. Your lender will hire an appraiser to view the property and complete a report to determine the property value. Also, on an investment property, they will assess appropriate rental rates. All of this is often just another step in the process, but if the value of the appraisal comes in under the contract price, it can mean more negotiations with the seller. Also, during the under-contract process, you will need to contact insurance to get a policy issued on the property you are purchasing. You can bundle your investment property with your personal residence and auto. Don't forget to obtain personal liability insurance also. We will cover more about insurance later in the book.

We are now in the home stretch of the purchase. The lender will send the final figures to the title company and you. Once you know the final amount needed for closing, you will need to obtain wiring instructions to wire the funds. Ensure that you call the title company for instructions regarding wiring the funds and do not accept wiring instructions from anyone else. Fraud is rampant, and if you receive instructions from someone other than the title company, the wiring instructions may direct your funds to a thief's offshore account. Be careful.

Prior to closing, it is wise to do a final walk-through of the property. The purpose of the walk-through is to ensure that the property is in the same condition that it was when you wrote the contract. This is a good time to verify that the seller has completed the inspection items you requested be repaired or replaced.

Closing day! The long-awaited day has arrived. You have wired your funds to the title company. Bring your ID to closing and be ready to sign documents. Now it is time to celebrate. You are beginning your journey as a landlord.

A Helpful Hint! Closing day is an exciting day. It is easy to get caught up in the moment and not get the necessary information that you will need after closing. In addition to the keys, make sure that you get the code to the garage door keypad if necessary. Learn where the mailbox is and get keys to the box if needed. If you purchase a property where the HOA covers trash service, find out what day is trash day. The seller is a great one-time resource, so make sure to get as much information from them as possible. Ask about the neighbors and any neighborhood tidbits like community events, who has the barking dog, and who is generous with garden produce. These are all good things to know.

If you are purchasing a property where tenants already live, make sure that you are given contact information for your tenants. After closing, set up an appointment to meet them. This appointment will be a meet and greet. Remember that you are required to honor the lease in place and cannot make changes.

Depending on the state where you purchase property, the process may be slightly different; the process outlined here is for a good funds state. The process in an escrow state could be slightly different. You now own a property that you plan on using as a rental. What is next?

Chapter 10

I Am a Landlord—Where Do I Start?

Congratulations! You are the new owner of a property you plan to use as a rental. Whether this property is your first rental property or your tenth, the following information and helpful hints can come in handy. As with anything, little details can make a big difference between being successful or frustrated as a landlord. Below is a list of things you will need to do to establish your rental business.

One of the first steps is setting up a new bank account specific to this rental. Start the account with $500 in it. When you get your security deposit from the tenant, deposit it into this account, and ensure the account balance does not drop below the amount of the security deposit. All rental checks should be deposited in the account once received. Tenants appreciate prompt deposits of checks. Whenever you have an expense for the rental, the expense comes out of that same account. It would be best to get a debit card for the account. Then when you have to go to your local home improvement store to purchase something for the rental, you can use the card to pay and have the money come directly from that account. It makes bookkeeping easy, and you will have an easier time with taxes next year.

Another important step in the process is to get signed up for a tenant screening service like RentPrep. Many companies provide this type of service. Services include credit and background checks on your prospective tenants. Do your research and pick your favorite. Then, when a prospective tenant comes to view your property and expresses interest in renting the property, you can direct them to the website where they fill out the rental application.

Once the prospective tenant completes the application, RentPrep, or another service, collects the application fee, runs the credit check and background check then provides you with a report regarding the prospective tenant. Information regarding the prospective tenants' background and credit is vital. The latter tells you about how they handle finances, and the former is about how they handle their lives.

Set up your screening criteria that will be used for all prospective tenants. As a part of that criteria, you will set minimum allowable credit scores in the system. I suggest a range of 700 to 720. You can decide. How do you decide the number for the minimum credit score? Below is the range for credit scores to help you evaluate the general risk, given the prospective tenant's score. For example, if your tenant was buying a home rather than renting from you, the minimum required credit score for conventional financing is 620. Most mortgage lenders consider credit scores of 740 or higher to be exceptional.

Credit score ranges
- 800-850 Exceptional
- 740-799 Very good
- 670-739 Good
- 580-669 Fair
- 300-579 Very poor

You will be required to answer many other questions to set up your criteria, including whether you are interested in background checks that include looking at criminal history. You may feel that this goes too far and is not really necessary. Think again. By using a screening service that provided me with a background check, I learned that a gentleman who had submitted an application for my rental had just been released from jail. He had served time after being found guilty of domestic violence. The prospective tenant and his soon-to-be ex-wife were separated, but they had a daughter, and the couple would be in regular contact with each other for visitation. I did not want that happening in or around my rental.

I told him, as you should in this situation, "Your rental application was rejected." He accepted that simple explanation. If you have a prospective tenant that does not accept that explanation and presses for why, you can say, "Due to background check" or "Due to your credit scores." Do not provide detailed information. In this situation, the less you say, the better. Using an outside screening service takes the decision out of your hands as to whether or not a prospective tenant is acceptable. If needed, you can refer the prospective tenant to the screening service to get their detailed questions answered. The screening service that you select should provide a phone number that your prospective tenant can call to get questions answered regarding the rejection of their application.

A Helpful Hint! *Everyone* over the age of eighteen that will be living at the property should be required to complete an application.

Another critical step in setting up your rental business is calling utility providers and getting accounts set up with the property address in your name. You do this so that you can be informed about non-payment, late payments, and potential shut-offs. Most utility providers will set up the account so that you can be notified if your tenants are behind in payments, or you can also be notified if the tenant is at risk of the utilities being shut off for lack of payment. You can also have the utility, rather than shutting off the service for lack of payment, put the service into your name. You are notified when this is about to occur. This transfer is not done when the tenant is late with a payment. Instead, this switch of the utilities into your name occurs after months of non-payment, and the utility is planning a shutoff. Having the utilities put in your name rather than shut off will limit the possibility of damage to the property due to frozen pipes or lack of water. Once you are notified by the utility provider that your tenant has not been paying for utilities, your lease should cover what should happen next.

You have taken the first steps to set up your rental business. Next, we will cover in more detail what to do to get your rental rented.

Chapter 11

Getting Started—What to Do to Get My Property Rented

The first step to getting your place rented is to advertise your rental. Where do you advertise your place for rent? It is important to give your property as much exposure as you can. I like to combine old-fashioned advertising mixed with new online technology advertising. First, put a FOR RENT sign in the window. The sign is advertising and directional help for prospective tenants to find the property when they come to view it. Next, advertise your property online; many different websites are available. Each will bring a different quality and type of tenant.

> **A Helpful Hint!** If you are purchasing a property and do not yet own it, you will not be able to advertise on Zillow. You'll need to wait until you are the owner of the property.

I recommend avoiding Craigslist. Of the other websites, Zillow can be one of the best for the individual property owner. Zillow will get you a lot of traffic and clicks on your advertisement, but you cannot put all of the information on the property, so you have to screen people once they call. For example, through Zillow, they will not know if you accept pets or the lease terms. Another advantage to advertising on Zillow is that other websites pick up information from Zillow and publish it on their sites. HomePad is one of those sites that take ads from Zillow and republishes them on their site. Facebook is another possibility. Most people do not look for their next place to live on Facebook, but it is another place for exposure to your rental. The more exposure you have, the more likely it is to get it rented. Remember that your prospective tenant may not see the ad, but their friend might and tell them about the rental. You never know how many times your ad might be shared. Do old school like the sign in the window and web exposure. Word of mouth is important too. Tell your friends, tell your neighbors and co-workers that you have a place for rent. You never know how you might find your next tenant. Each source of advertising can bring you a different quality and type of tenant. Once people reach out to get more information about your rental, it is important to screen them. It is nice to know how they learned about the rental. That is a good first question to ask. Then you have some idea of what they might know and can start by telling them more information and asking lots of questions about them and what they are looking for.

A Helpful Hint! Did you know that when you list a property for rent on Zillow, they provide you with what they think you should be charging for rent on the property? This can help you arrive at an appropriate price for the monthly rent. I recommend that you do not try to charge more than the amount that Zillow is estimating. Tenants see that suggested rental rate and feel that more is unfair to them.

Now you know a bit about the prospective tenants. Ideally, while you have them on the phone, do some screening before setting an appointment to view the property. Consider weeding out people that have pets or do not want a place right away. Use the information in the chapter "Twenty Questions to Ask Potential Tenants" to screen prospective tenants—you don't need to ask every question on the list, but certainly, ask about pets and how soon they need a place to live.

It is also good to ask about income to ensure that the prospective applicant's monthly income is at least three times the monthly rent. This benchmark, or standard, is used by property management companies and mortgage companies to ensure that housing expenses are not more than thirty-three percent of the prospective applicant's monthly gross income. You may want to use similar ratios as a guide when establishing whether a prospective tenant will be able to pay the rent each month.

As an example: If your current monthly rent cost is $1,000, you need to verify that the prospective tenant makes at least $3,000 a month. Make sure that they are comfortable having a background check run and a credit check done. You will need to ask these questions of potential applicants specifically. You will also need to decide if you will allow for a co-signer. Prospective tenants may want to use a co-signer for several different reasons. Perhaps their credit scores are below your minimum; their income is too low, or they have no credit. You may be asked this question about co-signers; make sure you are confident with your stance before showing your property. A co-signer is responsible for the rent if the person living in the property cannot pay. If you decide that you are comfortable with a co-signer, the co-signer will also need to complete an application and be approved along with the person living there.

A Helpful Hint! Rather than asking if a prospective tenant has pets, instead ask, "How many pets do you have?" With this question, you are more likely to get an honest answer.

The next step is to schedule a time to show the rental to prospective tenants. Know that during this process, you will have appointment no-shows. It is part of the rental game and to be expected. Asking questions and pre-screening over the phone will minimize no-shows. Some landlords call or text to remind the potential tenant of the appointment; whether you do this is up to you. They are adults. I prefer to treat them as such, and I do not remind them of the appointment.

It is wise to set appointments with prospective tenants at close to the same time so that you can show the property to several prospective tenants on the same trip. For example, set one appointment for 5:00 p.m. and another at 5:15 p.m. You can also set appointments for the same time. The disadvantage of appointments scheduled simultaneously is that you do not get to spend as much time with the prospective tenant. You may miss out on the ability and time to ask them questions and find out what they are looking for and how your property measures up. The more information you can gain about a prospective tenant, the better.

If, after viewing the property, the prospective tenant is interested, you then provide them with the link to the online application to begin the application process. Ensure that all prospective tenants who express an interest in renting the property are provided with the link to the application. For most screening services, the process is as follows—once the link is provided, the prospective tenant logs on and provides the necessary application fee and then can complete the application. You may receive questions about the application as the prospective tenant navigates the application. Most screening services do not provide details about your rental. Thus, you are the only contact the prospective tenant has if they have questions. Be patient and take the time to answer whatever questions they have.

Continue showing the property to prospective tenants and having any interested person submit their application. Do not stop this process even if a prospective tenant says they love the rental and want it. They may or may not follow through with the application process or get rejected. You can collect applications from multiple prospective tenants simultaneously. Not all applications will be approved. Note the order in which the applications were received, and consider adopting the "first come, first serve policy" on applications. This can establish fairness in selecting a tenant. All applications are time and date stamped and are still subject to credit and reference checks.

Let prospective tenants know that you will accept the first person whose application, credit, and references prove satisfactory. As a part of the application process, your tenant screening service will run background and credit checks if you have requested this complete service. As applications come in, review the results provided by the screening service. Look at credit scores that are below your acceptable number and for past evictions. The reports provide you with all that information.

No matter how much information the tenant screening service provides about the prospective tenant, it is essential to do a bit of screening yourself. The screening service lets you know if the prospective tenant has ever been evicted, but there is more to learn. The current or previous landlord is the best person to provide you with much of this information. You are interested in the prospective tenant's payment history. Did they pay on time? Did they give proper notice when planning to move? Did they follow the landlord's rental policies? Did the tenant show consideration to neighbors, or were there problems? The most important question to ask the previous landlord is, "Would you rent to this person again?" The answer to that question could give you all the information that you need to know.

Once you have the application completed, the credit check and references received, and you have talked to the previous or current landlord, you should have sufficient information to decide about your prospective tenant.

You now know the process for getting your property rented. Now we will go deeper into the important details. Questions to ask your prospective tenant and how to write a riveting ad for your rental are covered next.

Chapter 12

Twenty Questions to Ask Potential Tenants

1. Do you currently rent? Tell me about your current rental.
2. How long have you lived in your current place of residence?
3. Why are you looking for a new place to live?
4. What date would you want to move in?
5. Tell me about what you do for a living.
6. What is a rough estimate of your income?
7. How many people would be living with you?
8. How many people living with you smoke?
9. How many parking spaces would you require if you rent here?
10. How many pets do you have?
11. Do you think your current landlord will give you a favorable reference?
12. Does your current landlord know you are considering moving?
13. Have you ever been evicted?
14. Can I tell you about my rental process?
15. Are there any issues I should know about before running a background screening for all the adults in the household?
16. Have you filed for bankruptcy in the last four years?
17. Will you be able to pay our lease application fee of ($ amount) if you fill out the application?
18. Would you be able to pay the security deposit of ($ amount) at the lease signing?
19. Are you willing to sign a one-year lease agreement?
20. Do you have any questions for me about the rental property

Chapter 13

How to Write a Compelling Ad for Your Rental

Writing a compelling ad is vital to getting prospective tenants excited about your property and getting it rented. Here is possible ad copy you might want to use for your rental condo:

> 2 bed, 1 bath condo for rent in Southeast Fort Collins. Available December 1st. $1500 a month, no pets, no smoking.

If you were looking for a place to rent, would you call on this ad? It might be the last place I called on to get more information. It does not tell much about the unit and certainly doesn't compel me to pick up the phone as soon as possible to see it. So, how do you write an ad that encourages prompt action?

Write a persuasive ad that lets the prospective tenant know you have something valuable to offer and motivates them to act to have it for their own.

Here are some things to keep in mind

- Position your property in your ad. Tell the prospective tenant how your place is better than everything else they have seen. What are the unique features? Is it the amazing location close to shopping and everything they need is within walking distance? Are you offering an amazing value, being priced less than what other properties are priced?

Remember to answer the question—what do you offer that other places do not? Think attention-grabbing!

- Remember who your tenant might be. Check demographics. An upscale young professional is interested in different things than a college student. Point out features to attract your desired demographic. This is not discrimination; this is marketing.

- Plan what to say. Your ad should be more than a flat presentation of facts. Use descriptive words. Remember to highlight important and appealing features. Make sure the words you use help the prospective tenant imagine themselves at home in your rental. Don't over-embellish. Make sure you are accurate in what you say, or you will have showings without the prospective tenant being interested. They will feel misled or disappointed. Make sure what you write is organized, clear, captivating and persuasive. Do not use phrases that discriminate—stay away from the following phrases, "Great family home. No students. Great for a young professional without children."

- Be sure to include any special expectations as a part of your ad. For example, do you allow pets or smoking? Do you require a credit and/or background check? Include the rent to income ratio that you require in the ad. What are the terms of the lease? Is it six month, one year, or month to month? This will keep some prospective tenants from applying. Saving you time and trouble.

- Never be satisfied with what you have written. Revise, edit and make sure you save your ad for the next time your rental is available.

- Don't forget to mention amenities in your rental ad and when prospective tenants come to look. A pool, tennis court or clubhouse can help your property stand out and may also justify a higher rental rate.

It is also valuable to have professional photos of your property. I know, I know, you think you have an i-phone or fancy smartphone, and it takes great pictures, and you don't need to pay someone. But what if you had amazing professional photos? You know the saying that a picture is worth a thousand words. In your photo collection, include photos of desirable things around the property and amenities that the tenant will have access to. Does your rental include a pool or workout facility or a nice park around the block? Get pictures and include them in the photos when advertising. Is your rental near a mall, popular restaurants, or a movie theater? If so, get a picture? Is "Old Town" nearby? Get a picture. Another thing about professional photos is that you have them and can use them repeatedly. It is money well spent and a business expense. Your photos are the first thing those prospective tenants will look at before deciding to set up an appointment to see your rental. It is your opportunity to make a good first impression.

If you have the property vacant when photographed, stage the property. If you do not feel comfortable or do not know how to stage, hire a home stager. They will put towels in the bathroom and situate décor around the property to add a feeling of warmth. They even hang pictures on the walls. All this will add to the appeal of a place. Real estate agents know that staged homes sell two to two-and-a-half times faster and for more money than un-staged homes. So, why wouldn't your rental rent faster and possibly for more money?

Here is an example of a fun, different ad that will make your prospective tenant smile and hopefully encourage prompt action.

Immaculate first-floor condo in MidTown Fort Collins seeks new tenants. Must love being close to walkable dining, shopping, the Max bus route, as well as a Cinemark Movie Bistro and XD theater. About me: I am a 2 bedroom 2 bathroom condo with new flooring, new paint, a gas fireplace, an in-unit washer and dryer, as well as central air conditioning. My primary bedroom has a walk-in closet and attached bath. I have a covered patio, and 1 car detached garage close by. About you: You are a non-smoker without pets (sorry, HOA policy). You pay utilities, but my owner takes care of the water and sewer, so no worries there. I am currently getting out of a relationship but will be available on November 1st. I look forward to meeting you!

Another important decision to be made before getting your place rented is establishing what you will charge for rent. The next chapter will address how to determine what you should charge.

Chapter 14

How Do I Determine What Rent to Charge on My Property?

It is helpful to know several pieces of information when determining the price you should charge for your rental. First, research the current vacancy rate in the community where your rental is located. By learning this, you are determining the demand for your rental. To sleuth out the answer, ask Google the following question, "Current vacancy rate in Fort Collins, Colorado," filling in your location for Fort Collins. You may also call local property management companies and ask what their vacancy rate is for rentals. If you are calling property management companies, call more than one to get a true picture. Some local newspapers will run articles about rental vacancy rates. Do your research.

In a balanced market, the vacancy rate is five percent. The lower the number, the better for landlords. Remember supply and demand. The lower the number of available rentals with high demand, the more interest there will be in your rental. If you have high supply and low demand, you will have less interest in your property. Searching that google page will let you know the vacancy rate, and in addition to that, you will find articles regarding the average rent for the community. What does the number regarding the vacancy rate mean? If that number is three percent, that means that for every one hundred rental properties, only three of those are available at any given time.

Next, to figure out what to charge for your rental, it is good to do additional research. For example, I like to check Zillow and other websites such as forrent.com and allpropertyservices.com for a picture of what others are charging in rent in my area. I look for comparable properties that have a similar number of bedrooms, bathrooms and similar square footage. Find out what websites are good to look at in the community where your rental is located and search those websites. Once I have done this research, I have a pretty good idea of what I should be charging. Remember that it is better to get less per month than to have the property vacant. Without a current tenant, you are missing out on rental income and are footing the bill for the property expenses yourself.

If you have "rent boosting" features that the other properties do not have, you may be able to charge a bit more per month. Rent boosting features can include neighborhood amenities such as a pool, tennis courts, or fitness center that your tenant would be able to use. Property features that can boost rent include an in-unit washer and dryer, stainless appliances, or solid surface countertops such as quartz or granite. Hardwood floors or fireplaces, particularly gas fireplaces, can also be considered rent boosters. Tenants love energy-saving features. If your property has energy-saving features, make sure your tenant knows. Those features can save them money, and it just might mean that you can get more for rent.

Northern Colorado is growing, and we have many people relocating here from all over the country. This was also the case when we had the housing crisis. No matter what seems to be happening in the country, Colorado continues to grow, and that means that there is demand for rentals. That demand is year-round but higher in the more desirable times of year to move, such as spring and summer.

You should select a price you would like to get for rent on your property. Prepare your ad and advertise your property. The market will tell you if you are too high. Often, if you are charging more than the market rent for your property, you will get no phone calls or very little interest in seeing the property. If that is the case, wait about one week, then reduce your rental amount. For example, if you are charging $1,000 and the phone doesn't ring, reduce the rental amount to $950. If you still have little interest at the end of another week, reduce again by $50. If your rental rate is more in the $2,000 range, you might try reductions of $100 until you get a tenant. Remember that it often costs less to charge less and get a tenant than it is to have your property vacant for a month. Keep this in mind when you are holding out for a higher monthly rental amount. You will often be costing yourself more in the long run. If you are getting phone calls and showings, be patient. It may just be a matter of finding the right person for your rental.

> **A Helpful Hint!** It is a good idea to charge $995 rather than $1,000 per month in rent. Psychologically, that amount seems like so much less than $1,000. If you want to charge $1400 for rent, ask for $1395. This pricing strategy is used in marketing all of the time.

You have now established what to charge on your available rental. Another important decision you should make is whether you will use a tenant screening service. We will cover the reasons why you should use a screening service in the next chapter.

Chapter 15

Should I Use a Tenant Screening Service?

Before we look at whether you should use a screening service, let's look at what a tenant screening service is. A tenant screening service is a consumer reporting agency that provides background data on tenant applicants. The data collected on your tenant applicant can include bankruptcies, judgments, liens, credit reports, sex offender status, criminal history, eviction history, and employment verifications. The report provided to the landlord provides a clearer picture of each tenant applicant. All tenant applications are handled the same, and the landlord is provided the same information about each prospective tenant. This information allows the landlord to evaluate tenant applicants before deciding on which prospective tenant to rent the property to. The cost of the service varies depending on the amount of information requested. The prospective tenant can pay for the service through an application fee.

Why should you use a tenant screening service? The major reason to use a tenant screening service is to protect yourself as the landlord. A tenant screening service makes it easy for you to treat all possible tenants equally and protects you from being charged with discrimination. Many tenant screening services are available; I use Rentprep. While I do not endorse Rentprep, I find it easy to use, and it works for me. Because of the multitude of options, you can choose the one that works best for you. There is no one perfect solution, and opinions about services vary greatly. The most important thing is to find one that you like and use it.

Make sure that the one that you choose has good customer service. Does the service have a phone number to call if you have questions? Try calling that number to see what happens. What are the hours of the service? It is important to know what their customer support is like. How long do they take to turn around a report? Does the tenant screening service offer different screening packages for you as the landlord to choose from? It is nice to have the ability to choose what you want to know about your prospective tenant. What happens when the prospective tenant wants to dispute inaccuracies? When evaluating what tenant screening service you will use, these are all good questions to ask!

A Helpful Hint! The Fair Credit Reporting Act (FCRA) requires that you provide the prospective tenant with notification that you will require a background and credit check. Furthermore, the prospective tenant needs to provide you with their written consent to obtain it. The prospective tenant has the right to dispute the report's findings and anything that they feel is inaccurate. The consumer reporting agency must correct any inaccuracies found in the report.

You have selected your tenant screening service and have determined the criteria used to evaluate your prospective tenant. What happens next? You will have the prospective tenant complete an application, and the information will be sent to your screening service of choice. The information is reviewed, and the prospective tenant is accepted or denied as a potential renter due to the information in their report. What happens if the prospective tenant demands a copy of the report? On top of finding a great tenant, now you have to help the rejected tenant get a copy of the report. This is when excellent customer service from the tenant screening service is essential.

A good tenant screening service will deal with the rejected tenant. Helping that rejected tenant get answers quickly can benefit you and protect you. The last thing you want is for your rejected tenant to Google "landlord discrimination" or "discrimination complaint for landlord." When someone does that Google search, they are just a couple of clicks away from filing a formal complaint for discrimination. You, as a landlord, can be charged with a civil penalty of $19,787 for your first violation of the Fair Housing Act. Most tenants do not know what could be included in a report. They can be quite surprised at the accurate, negative information reported about them. Providing them with that report quickly can defuse their anger and

Success Secrets for Landlords

help them realize the rejection was due to negative information about them, not you as the landlord being discriminatory.

You now have a clearer picture of the benefits of a tenant screening service. The next step is setting up what you would like to know about your tenant applicant and your criteria for evaluating the applications.

Chapter 16

Establishing Tenant Screening Criteria for Rating a Tenant

As discussed in the previous chapter, part of your rental business should be using a tenant screening service, which makes life easier and protects you from being charged with discrimination. The first step to using the tenant screening service is to establish what you will and will not accept in a tenant. The tenant screening services call this process establishing the criteria for screening.

To set these criteria, you will answer questions such as: Will you accept anyone who has filed for bankruptcy? What is the minimum credit score that you will accept? Will you rent to a convicted felon? How many late rent payments can your prospective tenant have had in the past? Will you allow someone that has broken a lease? This work may feel like it makes your screening process more rigid, but quality criteria are imperative for the success of your business. This process can also be called rental criteria or tenant selection criteria form. All these names can be used to describe the same process by different screening services.

A Helpful Hint! Most rental agencies and landlords have established that the tenant must have income that is three times the monthly rental amount. This is called the three-to-one ratio of income to rent, or around thirty percent of the tenant's total gross income. If the rent makes up too much of the applicant's monthly income, landlords worry that they will not be able to take care of the rent each month. Landlords do not want tenants to choose between paying rent and something else because their budget is too tight. Be sure to include income verification as a part of the tenant screening process.

Here is how this works. Your potential tenant fills out an application. The application is submitted to the screening service with their application fee, and your criteria work as the answer key to the test. They pass, or they fail. Before they submit an application, you can choose whether or not you provide the standards to your prospective tenants. Providing the standards you require may save you time in the end. If the potential tenant knows that you do not accept a credit score below seven hundred or that you do not accept anyone that has filed for bankruptcy, they may not apply, and they can avoid spending the money to submit an application that will be rejected. It is like telling potential tenants that you will not accept pets. That means any pets, not the cute puppy they just got or the fifteen-year-old cat that is so sweet. They know that their application will be rejected due to their low credit scores, the fact that they filed for bankruptcy two years ago, or because they have a beloved fur child. Both the potential tenants and you as the landlord can move on.

How can you use tenant screening criteria to defend a discrimination claim? Let's say that you have screened a tenant, and they have been rejected. They do not match or meet your criteria. The tenant feels that they have been discriminated against. It can take less than four minutes for a tenant to fill out a discrimination claim. Below are examples of potential claims.

They can say that they feel that they were discriminated against because:
- I have kids—rejected due to familial status
- Because I am black—rejected due to race
- Because I am Catholic—rejected due to religious beliefs

All of the above are protected classes, and if you are indeed rejecting a prospective tenant for any of these reasons, you can be in violation of Fair Housing.

The fines for a Fair Housing violation are steep.
- No Prior Violations: $19,787
- One Prior: $49,467
- Two or more Priors: $98,935

So, if you are found guilty of violating Fair Housing, you can be charged and forced to pay the above fines. These fines do not include other fees such as attorney and court costs. Now that I have your attention and you are a little scared, I imagine you would like to know how to prevent this from happening. How do you stay out of this kind of trouble? Good question. One that you certainly want to be able to answer! When you receive the phone call from HUD, this is what you should say:

"Oh yes, I remember Jane and her family. They did seem very upset when I told them that they were denied the rental. I provided them with the screening report that showed they did not meet the criteria. To be specific, they did not meet my rental history and credit requirements to be specific. Their credit scores were below my required seven hundred. That is why Jane and her family were denied the rental. I could show you a copy of my criteria if you would like." In this conversation you are clearly showing that you have a system and you have specific legal reasons why you denied them the rental.

You do not want to answer this phone call with, "I had a bad feeling about Jane and her family, so I decided to deny them the rental." Hopefully, this scenario will drive home the point that it is worth the time and trouble to use a tenant screening service and to set up your criteria with them.

Screening criteria is an excellent way for landlords to find the right tenants for their rental units, but if they do not follow the established rules and regulations, they can find themselves in a lot of legal trouble. Landlords should consult with an attorney to ensure that their tenant screening criteria are legal, fair and effective. With the right screening process, landlords can identify the best applicants and offer them a lease agreement. Next we will cover the details about the lease.

Chapter 17

Lease

The lease that you use is the *most important part* of your rental business; no other document is more critical than your lease. It is your protection if things go wrong. Your lease is also your guide on how to operate your business. There is no perfect lease or one that includes everything that you need. The best lease is written by a local attorney, preferably one who specializes in real estate law. This attorney should also be willing to work with you if there is a tenant problem.

Know that it is possible to have a well-written lease that is five pages, and other leases can be twice as long. A lease is like an ad that you write for your property; it should always be changing and updated. The lease should be added to and subtracted from as you learn how to protect yourself and cover potential problems. It can also change because local and state laws change, and your lease should reflect those changes. In a way, your lease is like the real estate contract for the state where you own property. Your lease should be reviewed by attorneys annually, and changes are made to keep the contract current, correct problem areas and make the document as clear and concise as possible.

Every lease needs certain elements. The most important element includes what is being rented, for how much, and for how long. The lease also needs to cover what is included—utilities, appliances, garage, amenities, and so on. The lease needs to detail the rent, how it is to be paid and to whom and when and what happens if it is not paid on time. The lease also needs to cover what happens if you receive a check without sufficient funds. How security deposits are handled also needs to be outlined. You should also include specifics on who is responsible for what, and what happens when the tenant does not do what is expected. The lease also needs to cover circumstances under which the landlord may enter the property. Details should include the notice required for entry and whether the tenant needs to be present.

Another essential element covered in a quality lease are rules and regulations. Some landlords decide to keep this element completely separate from the lease and have it as a document that the tenant signs in addition to, but not as part of the lease. This is a personal preference. The rules and regulations should certainly include important specifics that the tenant must do to comply with HOA rules if your rental is in an HOA. The rules and regulations can cover noise and basic property care such as lawn care, cleaning, snow removal, and so on. Everything in the lease needs to be very detailed so that everyone, landlord, tenant and attorney, understand the document and responsibilities so that there are no unknowns should a problem arise.

In Fort Collins, Colorado and some other Colorado Front Range cities, occupancy needs to be covered as a part of the lease or in rules and regulations. In the local market of Fort Collins, there is a "you plus two" rule (u+2). This rule outlines that no more than three unrelated parties may live together in a property. The city enforces this guideline, and if not met, the city will charge significant fines to both tenant and landlord. Authors note: To get a full explanation of (U+2), google: (U+2) Fort Collins. As a landlord, it is your responsibility to inform your tenants of this rule or similar rules depending on your locale and ensure that you are not renting to more than the maximum number of unrelated parties.

Another topic that needs to be covered in the lease is damage, which is a big topic and is best broken into damage and repairs. What happens if there is damage? What is considered damage, and what is normal wear and tear? Do you have the right to inspect the property during the lease period? What must you or your agents do before entry to the property? Must notice be given, or can the landlord enter with a knock? Repairs should be covered in the lease. The question of how long you have to complete the repairs should also be answered in the lease.

What happens if there is damage to the tenant's personal property? It is important that the tenant understands that your homeowner's insurance does not cover the tenant's personal belongings. The tenant's responsibility is to obtain renter's insurance that covers their belongings against theft or damage.

Violations should be covered in the lease, as well as move-out expectations. How much notice will the tenant need to provide prior to moving out? What are the expectations regarding post-occupancy cleaning of the property? Is the tenant allowed to make alterations to the property?

Another issue that can cause headaches for a landlord is parking. How many vehicles are the tenants allowed to have? Can the property be used for business purposes?

One other item that should be covered is what happens to the lease if a rental property is sold? A landlord cannot terminate a lease early because the landlord plans to sell the property unless the lease expressly gives that right to the landlord. The lease agreement is tied to the property, not to the owner. If the property is sold during the lease period, the tenant may live there until the lease expires. The new owner of the property has to honor all terms of the lease, including the lease's termination date and rental amount. If the new owner and tenant agree, only then can changes be made.

This information is by no way a complete list of questions that a well-written lease should answer. By covering a list of items that need to be a part of your lease, I am not suggesting that you write your own lease. *Please don't!* I am providing you with this information so that you can evaluate a lease that you obtain or that is written for you. Thoroughness and detail are the two primary factors needed in a successfully written lease.

You now understand that the lease is the most important document for a landlord, but what are the lease terms offered to the tenant? The next chapter will review the advantages and disadvantages of the typical terms offered.

Chapter 18

What Length of Lease Should I Offer?

The answer to this question is complicated, and truly, it depends. Leases are intended to protect the tenant more than they are the landlord. Some protections extend to the landlord, but for the most part, the protection of a lease benefits the tenant. A primary benefit of a lease is that the tenant knows that the lease terms will not change for the lease period. This means no rent increases.

In Northern Colorado, it is challenging to find a property that has a short-term lease. Even apartment complexes rarely offer three-month leases, and if they do, they are very expensive. When renting a property for a short period of time, like three months, the landlord can typically charge a couple of hundred dollars more per month during the short time that the tenant is in residence.

Some landlords believe that they should be able to divide the monthly rate by three and add that amount to what they would charge if the property were rented for one year. So, for example, if the rental rate was $1,000 for the property and you were offering the property for rent for three months, you might be able to charge $1,350 per month. The higher rate protects the landlord to a degree from the risk of having the property vacant until a new tenant can be found. To decide if it is worth the risk, the landlord should look at current vacancy rates in the community and the demand for short-term rentals.

What type of person wants to only live in a place for three months? Often, corporate relocations or people that have just moved to the area are interested in short-term rentals. This type of tenant wants to have some familiarity with the area before they purchase a property. A short-term rental gives them time to get acquainted with the area, find a property and close before the end of the lease. Honestly, what better tenants to have than someone that wants to buy a property? They will be in the unit a short time, have very little opportunity to cause damage, and be willing to pay more not to be locked into a long-term, one-year lease. They are interested in keeping their credit clean so that they can buy. That means they are more likely to pay rent and utilities on time. One thing that short-term tenants often have in common is that they are in transition.

Other options for lease periods are month-to-month, six-month, and one-year. The most common lease term is one-year. The benefit to the landlord is that they can rent it and forget it for almost a year until it is almost the end of the lease, and it is time to renew or find a new tenant. Generally, little time is required to maintain a one-year lease property. You collect the rent and manage repairs or problems. This is the reason that landlords like longer-term leases.

Finding a tenant can be labor-intensive. If you have a six-month lease, you may be finding tenants again in just six months. As mentioned above, make sure that you charge more in rent for a short-term lease to compensate for the effort put into finding a new tenant. Again, with a short-term lease, even six-months, you can usually charge more in rent. Not as much as with a three-month lease but a bit more. With a long-term lease, you can charge the going rate to a tenant for rent, with no upcharge for the shorter period.

A disadvantage to a one-year lease is that if you have problems with the tenant, you are stuck in a lease with them. You could buy them out, pay them for the rest of the lease period to get them to leave, or evict them if the problems are severe enough. Use the eviction option only as a last resort and have an attorney involved in the process. If you decide to try to evict your tenant without the help of an attorney, make sure that you follow all rules and regulations for your state when doing the eviction. More about evictions in a later chapter.

The other option for a lease period is month-to-month. This type of rental agreement is for only a duration of one month and is renewed automatically each month until either landlord or tenant terminates the agreement. A month-to-month lease is uncomfortable for landlords because of the shortness of the term and the tenant's ability to move with thirty days' notice. The lease should cover how much notice the tenant must provide before moving. Month-to-month leases are uncomfortable for tenants because they know that things can change each month, rent can increase, or other lease terms can change. Of course, the details of what a landlord can do and what changes can be made depend on the verbiage in the lease, as well as state and local laws. With a month-to-month lease, the landlord is not stuck with tenants. If the landlord is having problems with noise or late payments, the short-term lease means that the landlord can get different tenants quickly rather than putting up with the problems until the end of a long lease period or going through the eviction process.

Another reason to do a short-term lease is that your rental availability may have you trying to find a tenant at an undesirable time of year. It can be difficult to find a tenant in November, December or January, for example. Why not offer a six-month lease? This option has you finding a tenant at a better time of year, where you can, more than likely, charge a higher rate for the property and get it rented more easily. The tenant that you rented to in December may be interested in renewing when the lease expires in June. If this is the case, make sure that you renew for one year at that time so that you do not have the lease expire in December again.

I have offered a tenant an eighteen-month lease before, rather than doing a short six-month lease and renewing for a year at the end of six months. The tenant liked the idea and signed the lease for eighteen months. Make sure that you are comfortable with the tenant before doing this.

The lease period is up to the landlord. If you are willing to accept some risk, you could earn more rent by offering a short-term lease. Know that this may be more work because you are finding a tenant more frequently. If that idea does not appeal to you and you feel that the extra money is not worth it, then a longer lease, like one year, may be best for you.

As a successful landlord, inevitably, you'll encounter tenants with no credit history. The next chapter will address how to handle this situation when you are faced with it.

Chapter 19

The Prospective Tenant Has No Credit History

You have just shown your rental unit to a prospective tenant that you have a great feeling about. They have completed the application, and all looks good, but they have no credit score. None. Having no credit score is not the same as having poor credit, but it can be just as bad. The prospective tenant cannot show you that they are reliable. About one in five American adults either have no credit history or are unscorable. This means that 278,000,000 Americans will have trouble obtaining new lines of credit or may not be able to obtain housing if the landlord requires a minimum credit score. Let's explore how credit scores work.

A credit score is a numerical representation of an individual's credit history. So if a prospective tenant has no credit score, they may not have a credit history. No credit means that you haven't had any recent credit activity that the credit bureaus can use to generate a credit score. In contrast, bad credit results from mishandling credit and generates negative marks on your credit report.

So why would someone not have a credit score? The person could be young and not have used credit yet or had enough use of credit to establish information for a score to be generated. It often takes more than a few months to create a score. Lenders are not required to report account activity to the credit bureaus regularly. Most do, but it is not required. Or, the person could be older, be free of debt, and pay for everything with cash. In this case, the older person would also not have a credit score.

How is a credit score calculated? There are two major credit reporting agencies. One is Fair Isaac Corporation, known as FICO, and the other lesser-known company is VantageScore. Each calculates scores differently, and each has different minimum requirements.

FICO's basic requirements are:

- One credit account with reported activity in the last six months — this could be on a loan or a credit card.
- One credit account older than six months.
- No record that the account holder has died.

VantageScore can generate a score after only one month of credit activity.

Credit scores are important because they determine an individual's financial responsibility. The person's credit score shows their credit trustworthiness. Without that score, it is difficult to determine the risk. There is no recorded history of repaying debts. In many ways having no credit score is the same as having a poor credit score because you have no proof that the person repays their debts or how timely the repayment occurs. Given this situation, you could decline the application that has been submitted. The prospective tenants do not meet the minimum credit score required because they have no score.

If you would like to research this tenant further and are considering giving them a chance, how do you evaluate the risk? Take a look at their bill payment history. For example, you could request to see their payment history of utility and cell phone bills, or if they have rented in the past, you could request to be provided with the payment history of their rent. Another way of checking the prospective tenant's ability to pay is to look at the cash flow in their checking account. This will require that they provide you with bank statements for two to three months. These statements will show you if they ever had an overdraft, the average amount of cash they had available at any given time in the account, and if bills are paid on time.

The prospective tenant has to be willing to be transparent and work with you to provide this information. If — for any reason — you cannot obtain this payment history, it is a good chance that the prospective tenant is not worth the risk. An option in this situation is to ask the prospective tenant if they have someone that would cosign with them. A cosigner can make it possible for the prospective tenant to rent the property and provide you with another person to collect from if the rent is not paid. The cosigner will be required to apply just like they will be living there and will need to have the application approved. The cosigner will be responsible for the rent if not paid by the tenant living in the rental. You must have the cosigner's complete contact information in case you need to contact them due to unpaid rent. The final decision is yours. If you are not one-hundred percent comfortable, remember to be patient and wait for another tenant.

You have had applications submitted to your screening service by prospective tenants. Additionally, you have reviewed the applications. What are the next steps in the process? The next chapter will cover allowable reasons for rejecting a tenant application, how to choose from the acceptable applications and determine who your next tenant should be.

Chapter 20

Choosing a New Tenant

If you are lucky, you will have several applications to choose from when you advertise your property for rent. Now it is time to decide who your new tenant will be. In many ways, the decision will be based on your own judgment. You will eliminate the prospective tenants that have poor credit or have had an eviction. They are easy to eliminate. Beyond that, let's go into specifics about whom you should reject and the valid, legal reasons for rejecting a tenant's application.

The following is a list of valid reasons for rejecting an application

- The prospective tenant's income is not three times the rent. The three times the rent is a guide frequently used by property management companies. This guide works for determining if a prospective tenant can afford a rental.
- Negative references from previous landlords, which may include excessive damage upon moving out, late rent payments, problems with neighbors, late utility payments, or eviction.
- Low credit score or poor credit history. If the prospective tenant's credit score falls below the credit score you have determined as acceptable, they are rejected. You must tell the prospective tenant how the credit information was obtained so that they can dispute the accuracy of the credit report if they choose to do so. This is their legal right and a requirement of the Federal Fair Credit Reporting Act.
- The prospective tenant cannot meet the obligations of the rental lease. For example, they have a pet, and you have a no pet policy, or they want a different lease term than you offer.

- The prospective tenant does not meet the background check. This can be due to a criminal offense. You are not allowed to reject someone for a drug use conviction but can reject for selling or manufacturing or currently using illegal drugs or involvement in violent crime.
- The prospective tenants want to exceed occupancy limits that are allowed by your lease or the municipality where the property is located.

A Helpful Hint! You *must provide* the name, address, and phone number of the credit reporting agency that provided you with the negative credit information on your prospective tenant. The declined prospective tenants have the right to receive an adverse action report from the credit reporting agency.

Now the hard part is sorting through the qualified applicants that seem acceptable. How do you select the best or the right tenant? In the case of evaluating which tenant is best, it would be ideal for prospective tenants to have most if not all of these qualities.

Desired qualities for your prospective tenant
- Sufficient income—the industry standard is three times the monthly rental rate.
- No criminal record.
- Meet or exceed the minimum credit score that you have set.
- Good references from past landlords.
- No evictions.
- Complete rental application.
- Able to meet the lease terms—length of the rental term, no pets, good references.

Once you have evaluated your prospective tenants using the above guide, you should be able to select your tenant. If more than one tenant is acceptable, you may use the first-come, first-serve method to decide between them. If you use this method for your final selection, some of the decision-making will be done for you. This method is usually accepted as "fair" by tenants that are found to be acceptable but do not get the property.

A Helpful Hint! When you are done using a consumer report or credit report, you must securely dispose of the report. This can be done by burning or shredding the document so that it cannot be read or reconstructed. Also, make sure that you dispose of electronic information that was obtained. This is required to comply with the Fair Credit Reporting Act.

Once you have an acceptable application, your next step is to properly deny applicants you choose not to rent to. It is vital to remember to say very little when providing the notification. Examples include, "Your application was denied due to credit," or "Your application was denied due to the background check." If they ask why they're denied, have them call the 1-800 number of your tenant screening service, and the screening service will answer any additional questions and take the pressure off of you. This is another great reason to use a screening service.

Not all screening services make it possible for your denied tenant to call them for further explanation. Before selecting a specific screening service, make sure that they provide this support. Having the denied tenant call a 1-800 number can make a potentially uncomfortable situation much easier for you to deal with. The denied tenant may have no idea they have poor credit. It is valuable to the denied tenant to be offered a detailed explanation by the screening service. It can be the first step in making it possible for them to clean up their credit report or information on their background report.

A Helpful Hint! Within your application pool, if you do not have an acceptable tenant that meets your qualifications, do not lower your standards and select the least objectionable one. Instead, repeat the process until you have an acceptable tenant. You will thank yourself for being patient and waiting for the right one.

The final step in renting your property is setting up a meeting with the new tenant for lease signing, collecting the security deposit, and handing over keys. Read "Steps to Setting up a New Tenant" for more information.

In review, below is the process of getting your property rented

- Advertise the rental.
- Prescreen prospective tenants over the phone.
- Show rental.
- Provide a link to the application.
- Review applications.
- Select your new tenants.
- Notify your approved tenant.
- Properly deny applicants that you did not choose.

- Set up a meeting with your new tenant for lease signing.

As part of finding a new tenant, it is very important to keep some things in mind. Every prospective tenant *must* be treated the same. All that request an application must be given an application or a link to an application. All applications received must be processed. You do not ever want to be accused of discrimination.

Below are seven protected classes that you need to be aware of.
1. Race
2. Color
3. Religion
4. National origin
5. Gender
6. Familial Status
7. Mental or Physical disability

Number seven is a tough one. It can be difficult to tell that someone has a disability. You are not in a position to judge. If the prospective tenant tells you that they have a disability, believe them. If you need proof—for example, if the tenant needs a therapy dog—ask for proof. Some people use therapy dogs for gaming the system. They say that they *have* to have a therapy dog or other comfort animal, and therefore the dog must be allowed even though you have a no pet policy. Be careful. Make them prove via a doctor's letter stating that they *need* a dog or another animal for their mental or emotional well-being. I have not run into this, but I have had clients that have. The prospective tenant could not produce the letter, and the dog was not allowed.

Following a consistent system when finding tenants will minimize the risk of being accused of discrimination. Finding the right tenant may sound scary, but if you follow your system, you will have nothing to worry about.

Next, we will cover what to do after selecting a tenant. As previously discussed, you have let prospective tenants know that you will not rent to them, saying little during the rejection conversation. You have provided the contact information for the reporting agency that provided you with the information that caused the denial. Remember, the more you talk, the more you need to be careful about possible discrimination issues.

Now you get the fun of calling your approved tenant and letting them know the good news. Their application was accepted. Then what? That will be covered next!

Chapter 21

Steps to Setting Up a New Tenant

You have found the perfect person, and you are ready to get them moved in and wind down this part of your job as a landlord. You are ninety five percent of the way to having your property rented! Once you have determined which prospective tenant you will accept, it is time to let the tenant know. Call them and tell them you would welcome them as a tenant.

Sometimes surprises happen. Once, when I made this phone call, I learned the tenant had already found another place. I have also had an instance where the prospective tenant is trying to decide between my rental and another one. Remember to be patient. This is not the time to start negotiating terms or rent, even if they ask.

At this point, go over the terms again, saying, "Remember that the rent is $1,000 a month and will need a $1,000 security deposit. I will need you to provide me with a certified check or money order for the amount of the rent and security deposit when we meet." As a landlord, you should only accept certified funds for the first month's rent and security deposit. "I will accept a personal check after this point for rent but must have a certified check or money order for deposit and first months' rent. Also, please remember that anyone over the age of eighteen that will be living in the property will be signing the lease." You should provide a copy of the lease for the tenant to review before the appointment. This can be done by email. Suggest that the tenant review and ask any questions before the appointment.

Set up an appointment for lease signing, and let the tenant know that they need to allow an hour for this appointment. At this appointment, provide the tenants with contact information for the utility providers. Create a one-page document that includes contract information for electricity, water, sewer, and natural gas providers, as appropriate. You can also include available cable internet choices. This is helpful information that the renter will need, and if you do not provide this information, they may ask. Providing the information makes it easy for them to make phone calls to start service. Let them know that they need to have the utilities in their name within forty-eight hours of signing the lease or whatever time frame that you have as your policy.

Also, provide the tenant with a couple of phone numbers for insurance agents. This shows them that you care about their personal property and possessions, and it clarifies that your homeowner's insurance does not cover their personal belongings.

A Helpful Hint! Remember to call utility providers for the property and tell them that you own the property, though renters will be paying the regular bills. Set up an account for the property so that if the utility is going to shut off the service, that utility provider will instead put the utilities in your name. Inform the utility providers that you would like to be notified if the tenant is behind in their payments and could be facing a shut-off.

For the lease signing appointment, bring the lease, keys, garage door opener, keys to amenities and parking permits. At this appointment, walk the tenant through a move-in inspection. During the move-in inspection, the tenant will note any current damages to the property. It is a good idea to take photos of any damage found. Let the tenant know that they will be responsible for any damages not found at this time. This will usually motivate them to take the time to really look around. You might even find damage that you were not already aware of.

It is time to sign the lease. In my experience, it is a rare tenant that reads the lease. Thus, it is a good idea to review the lease with the tenant. Hit the high points and answer any questions. I remind tenants that I follow the lease to the letter. That way, they know exactly what to expect. I use the example of the rent payment being late. The lease outlines exactly what will occur. I offer no second chances; if the tenant is late, the lease says what you are to do. Provide detailed directions for rent payments. Do you want the rent check to come via mail, or is it to be dropped off at a specific location? Does the rent check have to arrive by the deadline dates in the lease or just be postmarked by the dates? If you accept automatic withdrawal or automatic payments from the tenant's bank, discuss this option with them.

In this situation, the tenant provides you with their bank account information, and your bank auto deducts the rent payment from their account on a certain date each month. This is by far the easiest for all parties.

Provide the tenant with your contact information and directions on what to do if something breaks or if there is an emergency. Provide the tenant a signed copy of the lease and keep a signed copy for your records. Also, have the tenant fill out a "tenant info sheet," which includes their contact information, including email, cell number, and a person to contact in case of emergency.

The signing appointment is a great time for tenant orientation. Demonstrate how to use the furnace, A/C, appliances, and any other idiosyncrasies of your property. Review the services such as trash, recycling, and any neighborhood conveniences. If they are new to town, let them know about the closest grocery store. Share details about a great nearby coffee shop and your favorite local places to eat.

The lease is signed. The tenants have provided you with a list of damages, and you have been provided with the certified rent check and security deposit. Your tenants have agreed to put the utilities in their name within forty-eight hours. It is time to hand over the keys. Additionally, you have accomplished the hardest and most important part of being a landlord, finding a good tenant and completing the process of getting your investment property rented. Congratulations!

Chapter 22

Tenant Expectations

You now have someone living in your property. What do you expect of your new tenant? They've done a walk-through with you looking for existing damage and learning how to use various appliances and features. Additionally, show them how to do some basic home maintenance. These things can minimize damage to the property if there is a problem.

Below is a comprehensive pre-move-in checklist
- Show them the main water shut-off for the property, and point out the individual shut-offs for sinks and toilets.
- Show them how to shut off the gas service to the property.
- Show them how to change the furnace filter.
- Show them how to unclog the garbage disposal.
- Show them where the electrical panel is and how to reset a breaker.

Ensure that the tenants understand that you are not expecting them to do maintenance on the property, but you feel they should know these basic things and then call you. Tell them that this is just good stuff for them to know when they buy their own home someday. They may laugh at you, but they will get the idea.

In addition to showing them how to do these items, let the tenant know your expectations of their responsibilities. This list can be changed, added to and subtracted from based on your property and what you want from your tenant. This list, though not comprehensive, offers a beginning template of expectations for your tenant. Adjust as necessary.

Tenant expectation checklist

- Snow is to be removed from sidewalks within twenty-four hours after the end of a snow storm. This may not be your rule and may be based on the rules in the municipality where your rental is located.
- The lawn needs to be kept green and mowed regularly. Some municipalities can fine the owner of the property if lawns are not well kept. Do your research and make sure you know what rules apply to your rental based on location.
- Tenants need to get renters' insurance. It can cost as little as $10 a month. Your homeowner's insurance does not cover anything but the property, and the tenant's personal items are not included. The tenants' belongings are only covered if they have their own renters' insurance policy.
- Only minimal toilet paper goes down the toilet. No Q-tips, no feminine hygiene products, nothing but toilet paper—even items described as flushable. If the sewer system gets plugged and items other than toilet paper are found flushed down the toilet, the tenant will be responsible for the cost of cleaning out the sewer line. Often this cleaning fee is several hundred dollars. If the tenant cannot pay at the time of the event, it can be taken out of the security deposit at the end of the lease period.
- The tenant needs to call you as soon as there is a problem. If you are not notified of a problem, it may be considered neglect. Most problems only get worse over time, and proper notification can fix a problem before it gets worse.
- The area around the furnace is not for storage. This area is kept free of items so that the furnace can operate as intended.
- Central air conditioning is not to be set below 75 degrees in the summer. If the thermostat is set below that temperature, it will cause the system to freeze up, and the A/C will not cool the property.
- The thermostat is not to be set below 55 degrees in the winter.
- Only two cars are allowed to be parked on the property. (This is on a case-by-case basis and should be specific to your rentals' situation.)
- If the tenant plans to leave the property unoccupied for more than fourteen days, the landlord must be informed.

You get the idea of what could be on a list. I have referred to my list as Tenant Rules and Regulations. I have this list typed up, and it is presented to the tenant at the time of lease signing. I require that the tenant sign this form too. If your rental is in an HOA, it is advisable to provide your tenant with a copy of the Covenants, Conditions and Regulations (CC and R's). The tenant may not ever read them, but you have made them aware by providing a copy. At some point, if your tenant is not following the C, C and R's, you may receive notification from the HOA management company of a violation. After notification, you need to call the tenant and tell them that you have been informed by the HOA management company that they are not following the HOA rules. Your lease should cover what happens next.

As a landlord, you now have the experience of establishing the systems to get your property rented. You have navigated through the process of selecting a new tenant. The tenant has signed the lease and moved in. All appears to be going smoothly. Next, we will cover landlord responsibilities and what it takes to be considered a great landlord by your tenants.

Chapter 23

What Are the Legal Responsibilities of Being a Landlord?

Some laws have been created that serve as a guide for the rights and obligations of both landlords and tenants. State laws will vary, but all landlords must abide by a few general requirements. As a landlord, you are a business owner. Your first responsibility is to your tenant. Your property — where your tenant lives — is your asset and your tenants are your clients.

As a landlord, your responsibilities fall into four general categories
- Maintain your property so that it is safe, clean, and habitable
- Pay the property's bills, including mortgage, utilities, taxes and insurance
- Maintain records
- Manage security deposit provided by the tenant

As the landlord, you are required to take reasonable care of your property and to provide your tenant with a livable, safe, and clean place to live. Habitability law varies state by state, and it is your responsibility, as a landlord, to be aware of what these laws stipulate. In many cases, you are required to adhere to the municipality's building codes where the rental property is located. You need to perform necessary repairs. Major problems such as plumbing or heating should be handled within twenty-four hours. The landlord must provide notice before entering as written in the lease. Without notice, the landlord may enter the property if it is an emergency.

Beyond basic habitability requirements and doing repairs promptly, many states require that you provide your tenants with safe and hazard-free living quarters. It is not uncommon for older homes to be used as rental properties. These homes may have hazards such as lead or asbestos. This means if you cannot remove lead or asbestos from the property, you need to disclose that the property has those hazards in writing. By providing the disclosures, the landlord is protecting themselves, and the renter can make an informed decision whether they would choose to live in a property with lead-based paint, radon, asbestos, and so on. The federal government requires that before renting your property, you disclose if the property contains lead-based paint. If you do not disclose, you could face hefty financial penalties.

Most states also have requirements for the landlord to provide heat, electricity, and water—basic things that a landlord needs to protect their asset. Remember that you are required to provide your tenant with a safe place to live. This means maintaining locks and having locks changed between tenants. You also need to maintain a pest-free environment by handling any pest or vermin infestation. But your responsibility does not end there; this is just the beginning.

As a property owner, you are responsible for bills, including utilities, mortgage and taxes on the property. Your tenant is responsible for the payment of the rent, but it is up to you to keep the mortgage payments current. This sounds obvious, but it is important to mention. If you don't pay your mortgage, you could lose your asset, and your tenants could lose their place to live.

The landlord is ultimately responsible for paying the utilities on the property. You may have it set up so that your tenants pay them, but the utilities must be paid to protect the asset. Unpaid utilities can lead to damage. For example, how are the toilets being flushed if the water bill is not being paid and the water is shut off? If the utilities are not paid in some areas, this can create a lien on the property that will need to be paid when the property is sold. In some states, for example, water is a lienable item. The utility provider places the lien, and it sits on the property until the property is sold and then must be paid. As the landlord, you decide who is responsible for the various utilities. If you decide to make the tenant responsible for the trash, make sure that the trash is being removed from the property and that that bill is being paid. We have all heard stories of the landlord showing up to the property they own after the tenants have moved out, and the entire garage is filled with bags of garbage. Instead of paying for garbage removal, the tenants stashed it in the garage. Set it up with each utility that you are notified if utilities are being shut off due to lack of payment. By doing this, you can protect your asset from the possibility of frozen pipes.

As the landlord, you are also responsible for paying taxes on the property. Unpaid taxes can cause a property to be foreclosed on, just like if the mortgage is not paid. The town or county will foreclose for unpaid taxes. This is another unfortunate way to lose your asset, and your tenants lose their place to live.

The landlord is responsible for maintaining records. The most obvious record that the landlord needs to keep is the lease. The lease is the written agreement between the landlord and your tenant. The lease lays out the responsibilities of each party. If the landlord does not maintain a copy, there is no record of the agreement or each party's responsibilities. The landlord is also obligated to keep records of the rent payments that the tenant has made. This can be as simple as depositing the checks in the bank account and a receipt of the deposit being kept. If the tenant makes a rent payment in cash, provide the tenant with a receipt of payment and receive a record of the deposit from the bank. You should also maintain records on maintenance requests from your tenants and maintenance completed on the property. The final thing to keep a record of is any legal issues that have occurred.

The next responsibility of the landlord is to manage the tenant's security deposit. The landlord can charge the tenant a security deposit, but the security deposit does not belong to the landlord. The deposit is security in case the tenant doesn't pay rent or damages the property. The landlord must maintain the security deposit in an account. Specific state and sometimes local laws regulate security deposits—how much can be charged, what must be done with the deposit, and how soon it must be returned upon tenant move-out. Laws also cover what is to be done with the security deposit when the property is sold. A landlord that has collected a security deposit and is selling the property typically has two choices upon the sale. One is to return the deposit to the tenant. The other option is to transfer the security deposit to the new owner. Once the security deposit is transferred, the original landlord is relieved of any further liability.

It is also essential to know all of the landlord's responsibilities in the area where you operate your business. Be sure to consult with a real estate attorney, as needed, to ensure that you are kept current, as laws do change.

You now know what your legal responsibilities are, but what does it take to be a great landlord? This is covered in the next chapter.

Chapter 24

What It Takes to Be a Great Landlord

Better landlords have better tenants. As a landlord, it is important to remember that you are in business and providing a service to your tenants. Keeping this in mind, you can intentionally provide what your tenants need and retain long-term, qualified tenants. Considering the amount of time and effort it takes to find a great tenant—some estimates are between twenty and thirty hours, with advertising, showing the property, reviewing applications, going through the leasing process, lease signing, key exchange etc. Keeping a great tenant can save you hours of your time and unnecessary hassle.

So what does being a great landlord look like? Great landlords treat their tenants as customers; they follow the law and the lease. A great landlord is professional; they remember that they are running a business, and their actions reflect this. Little details mean so much and can make a difference in the tenant's impression.

Below are some tips on how to be a great landlord
- First and most important, provide your new tenant with a clean place to move into. This includes having the fridge and all other appliances sparkling. Make sure that carpets are professionally cleaned by a reputable company that does this for a living. Avoid renting a consumer-grade machine or one rented from your local grocery store. Providing your tenants with a clean property to move into reduces their stress and also sets the expectations of what you want the place to look

like when they move out. Conveying a clean property requires thinking ahead. Tenants may leave a property relatively clean, but not to the level of clean that you should provide the next tenant. Plan on hiring a cleaning service to give the property a once over. This will require scheduling the cleaning service and the carpet cleaner in advance. Depending on the schedule, this could mean that the property is vacant for a few days between tenants.

- Be warm and welcoming to your tenant. If they are new to the area, provide them with some helpful hints and ideas on local grocery stores, pharmacies, coffee shops, restaurants, and other things that might be important to them. You can create a one-page document to easily convey this information. You can use this repeatedly, so keep a copy on file for next time. Write them a warm welcome letter that thanks them for renting your place and welcomes them to the unit and the community. Let them know what day of the week is trash day and any other special instructions on the property. Also, provide parking information, including where to park and how many vehicles are allowed. As mentioned before, give them your contact information and provide them with the phone numbers of the utility service providers. Also, provide them with a copy of their new address. This may seem silly, but they need to know their mailing address, complete with the zip code. If this is quick and easy for you to do, provide them with a sheet of return address labels. These details show you care, are detail-oriented, and are responsible. Small details make a big difference.
- Stock the bathroom with toilet paper. This nice gesture will go miles in starting your relationship with your tenants off on the right foot. Also, place a roll of paper towels in the kitchen and provide a bottle of all-purpose cleaner. This shows them you care about cleanliness.
- Walk them through the lease. This is the agreement between the two of you. You need to know that they know what their responsibilities are. Review important sections. Walking them through the lease demonstrates that you are someone that is fair and that they can trust.

A Helpful Hint! As a landlord, you know it could take a couple of hours to go over every lease section. The new tenants' eyes will glaze over within a few minutes. So instead, bring a highlighted copy of the lease with you when you meet with the tenants for the lease signing. This will allow you to quickly refer to the important sections you want to review with the tenant and ensure that no important parts are forgotten or overlooked. Remind the tenant that they are responsible for knowing all information in the lease, but you are covering the highlights!

- Look professional by dressing neatly and looking your best at the lease signing. You want to provide a good impression. Those impressions mean a lot and speak volumes.
- Follow the lease. If there is ever a problem with a tenant, the lease is your guide on how to handle the problem. If, for some reason, your lease does not cover the problem, check with the local ordinances or check with an attorney on how it should be handled. A quick phone call to an attorney may cost you a few dollars but will let you know if you are within your rights. Connecting with a local landlord group provides an opportunity to get a response from another landlord. This response can give you an idea if you are consistent with other landlords.
- Always keep your cool! Whatever the situation, whatever the problem, keep your cool. Never yell or swear at your tenant. Remember, the tenant is your customer, and you are providing a service.
- Tenants are not your friends. A friendly professional relationship is fine but draw the line there. At the end of the day, remember that this is a business relationship. It is important to keep that emotional distance in case there is ever a problem, and you have to take them to court.
- Be consistent. *Always* follow the lease to the letter. That is the agreement between the parties, and it needs to be always followed. That means if they are late with the rent, no matter what the story, no matter what the situation, "the lease says." Be respectful and be consistent. Let the tenant know that you always follow the lease, and you will be seen as professional. This also means that the tenant can look at the lease and know what to anticipate from you!
- Be accessible. If your tenant needs to reach you, you need to be reachable. Respond promptly when your tenant calls or emails. Remember that this is a business. If you are going out of the country or plan on being unavailable for a period of time, let your tenant know what to do in case of an emergency. Provide them with a contact person who can handle your business while you are away. You also need to provide instructions to the contact person. For example, let both parties know what you would like done in a mechanical emergency. This contact person provides a service to your tenant and needs complete information. If you have a list of service providers that you use, that

information should be a part of the packet of instructions. Also, provide a copy of the lease and any additional special instructions.

A Helpful Hint! A small welcome package won't cost very much and maybe just the perfect thing to start your relationship with your new tenant off on the right foot. Be sure to include a personalized note, and other items that could be included in the package are:

- A couple of rolls of toilet paper
- A roll of paper towels.
- A container of Clorox wipes.
- A scented candle or flowers.
- A few bottles of water in the refrigerator.
- A 6-pack of your favorite local beer, if tenants are over twenty-one years old, of course!
- $5 gift card to your favorite local coffee shop.

One of the important steps in the process of being a landlord is setting up a new tenant and handling the transition between tenants. Tenant move-out is a part of that transition. This topic is covered in the next chapter.

Chapter 25

Tenant Move-Out

The most important times in the life of a Landlord are the times that they interact with their tenants. An interaction handled correctly can keep things between the landlord and tenant going smoothly. If the interaction is done incorrectly, it can have lasting negative impacts on the landlord. One of these instances can occur when the tenants move out.

Approximately forty-five to sixty days before the end of the lease, it is wise to contact your tenants and find out their plans. If they plan to renew the lease, it is important to get the new lease to them to sign promptly. It is wise to let the tenant know that you expect the signed renewal lease to be returned before the end of the current lease. However, it is best to make sure to have it returned a minimum of two weeks before the end of the current lease. I prefer to have it returned thirty days before the end of the lease period.

If, instead of renewing, your tenant has informed you that they plan to move out at the end of the lease period, what do you do? You now prepare for tenant turnover, which is discussed in detail in the Tenant Turnover chapter.

As always, it is beneficial to have a system in place and handle finding new tenants the same way every time. You have a choice. Your first choice is to show the property to prospective tenants while the current tenant is occupying the property. You will have to coordinate showings and schedules. You will need to provide notice to your current tenant for showings, and how much notice depends on the lease details. Some leases require twenty-four-hour notice; some don't. Your other choice is to wait until your tenant moves out and show the property to prospective tenants when it is vacant.

The choice is yours and may depend on how well the property shows with the tenant in it. If the property does not show well because it is overstuffed with furniture and tenant's belongings or if the tenant is not tidy, it may be wise to wait. You want to attract the best future tenant to the property. The best way to achieve this is to have the property show its best when the prospective tenants come to view the property.

A couple of weeks before the end of the lease, check in with the tenant to make sure that they have found a place to move to and their schedule for move-out. Remind them of your expectations regarding moving out, whatever they are. Remind them of the date and time for the expiration of the lease. Do not let them stay past that date and time, even if they are cleaning. Schedule a time to meet them to have the keys returned. It is important to walk through the property and find out if there is anything that the tenant had had problems with during the time that they lived there. Note any damage that they point out—damage is anything not considered normal wear and tear. Lastly, be sure to get the tenants' forwarding address!

Remind the tenants that the security deposit will *not* be returned on move-out day. Inevitably you'll have expenses post-move-out, which will come from the security deposit—see the list below. You need to spend some time in the property verifying that everything works and that there is no additional damage. Any damage needs to be photographed and then repaired. Many landlords develop a checklist so that they can go down the list and know what they have looked at and what they still need to inspect. If you develop a checklist, devise a rating system regarding the overall condition. For example, very good, good, fair, needs to be repaired or replaced. The carpets will also need to be cleaned. The lease that I use states that the carpets will be *professionally* cleaned after moving out. That means someone with a truck that does this for a living, not the tenants' carpet cleaning machine or a rented machine from the grocery store. Schedule carpet cleaning before the move-out day so that it can be completed promptly once the property is vacant.

Another important thing to do is to call the municipality that provides utilities to determine the remaining costs for water, sewer, and electricity. At the time of move-out, almost always, you will find a balance on the account. It is wise to wait until a couple of weeks after move-out to ensure that the utility provider is able to provide the amount for the *final* bill. Pay the final bill to the utility provider to close the account. That amount comes out of the deposit. In some municipalities, if the bill is left unpaid, the municipality will place a lien on the property, and when it comes time to sell, the lien will have to be paid by the owner of the property. Check the regulations in your area.

I once listed a property for sale that had been used as a rental for over twenty-five years. When the settlement statement was prepared prior to closing, we discovered nearly $2,000 in liens placed by the water provider for unpaid water bills over the years. The owner neglected to make that phone call for the final bill, and the water provider had placed multiple liens on the property. The seller had to pay the liens out of the proceeds from the home sale—not a pleasant surprise.

Provide the tenant with an itemized list of what money was deducted from their deposit and copies of receipts. Build into your lease that you have forty-five days in which to return the deposit. It should not take you that long to get everything done, but you do have that long if you need it. I like to make every effort to have it returned within thirty days. Tenants appreciate prompt repayment of the deposit, but don't let them rush you. Here is a list of reasons that you can withhold a security deposit.

A Helpful Hint! If you can, always use the same cleaning service or person for move-out cleaning. That ensures that the cleaning thoroughness and quality are the same every time.

You, as the landlord, may keep all or a portion of the security deposit for any of the following reasons.

Reasons to withhold a security deposit

- Unpaid rent owed by the tenant
- Unpaid utility bills
- Professional cleaning services, including carpet cleaning and services required to restore the unit to the condition found at move-in
- Any other breach of the lease causing financial damage to the landlord
- Payment for damages to the rental beyond "normal wear and tear"

A Helpful Hint! What is the legal definition of "normal wear and tear?" Colorado defines it as "deterioration which occurs based upon the use for which the rental unit is intended, without negligence, carelessness, accident or abuse of the premises or equipment...by the tenant or...household...or guests." C.R.S. $38-12-102(1) Be sure you know how your state defines the difference between normal wear and tear and damage!

Here are examples of the difference between normal wear and tear and damage:

Normal Wear and Tear	Damage
Faded, chipped paint	Hole in the wall
Worn keys	Missing keys
Dirty window blinds	Missing or broken window blind
Lawn mower needs the blades sharpened	Lawn mower that won't start or can't be repaired

Once the deposit is returned, your tenant may have questions. It doesn't happen often, but I know that it can. Make sure that you have good documentation, and you'll have nothing to worry about. Providing copies of receipts and an itemized list should minimize issues and questions. Tenants have a right to know what was deducted from the deposit, and you should always provide proof. Send the proof with the check.

Remember that repairs considered "normal wear and tear" should not be deducted from the security deposit. This will be the fastest route to small claims court for you as a landlord. It can be difficult to define "normal wear and tear." It is wise to tread cautiously on this topic. If it seems like excessive wear, think again before deducting it from the deposit. It may not be worth the trip to court.

A Helpful Hint! Colorado law requires that you *must* return the security deposit to the tenant within sixty days of the end of the lease, or the tenant move-out! Check the guidelines in your area. Mark your calendar and do not lose sight and forget. Check to make sure that you know how long you have before the deposit must be returned and stay up to date on any changes in the law.

One of the biggest mistakes I have made as a landlord was with a security deposit return. I had terrible tenants and was about to evict them for lack of rent payment. They moved in the middle of the night and saved me the trouble. I prepared the property for rent and made a list of all damages. The damages totaled more than the security deposit. The tenant had not provided me with a forwarding address. So, I did nothing. About sixty-five days after the tenant moved out, I received a letter from an attorney. I was told that I had five days to return the security deposit in full, or I would owe the tenant three times the security deposit. Rather than fight this, I returned the deposit and considered myself smarter.

ALWAYS send an itemized list of the damages and costs, including final utilities and cleaning costs, to the address of the property if the tenant did not provide a forwarding address. Copies of receipts should also be provided if you have them. That way, you are not in my shoes and providing a tenant with the full deposit when you are out more money than the deposit because of damage. Learning from my experience can save you money and heartache.

Chapter 26

Tenant Turnover

No, this isn't a delicious pastry. Tenant turnover is the process of transitioning a rental from one tenant to another. Turnover involves taking time between tenants to thoroughly clean the property and address any required improvements or maintenance needed to the property.

So, how long does the turnover between tenants take? It is not unusual for it to take one to possibly as long as two weeks. If you already have your next tenant ready to move in, the duration of your turnover needs to consider when your new tenants are supposed to take possession. The timeline can also depend on what needs to be done and how long your previous tenant has lived there.

Planning ahead can make a big difference. I suggest that you begin this process by setting up an appointment with your current tenants to see your rental property as soon as your tenants have notified you that they are leaving. Let your tenant know that you want to look around and have them show you what needs attention. This walk through helps you solidify what needs to be done after the current tenant moves out. Are you going to need to paint? Will you need to replace the flooring, or is cleaning carpets and a good general cleaning enough? This is your time to attend to property maintenance which is difficult to do when someone is living there. Make a comprehensive list of tasks that must be done. Below is a checklist of things to consider when preparing the property for your next tenant.

Turnover checklist
- Is the property clean? When I ask this question, I mean incredibly clean. Move-in ready. This includes appliances, windows, and blinds. You

will more than likely need to hire a professional cleaner or cleaning service. Depending on how many people are working to clean and how dirty your tenants left the property, this may mean a couple of hours of work to a whole day. If you do this every time you switch tenants, you can charge the tenant the cost of cleaning if the property is not left as clean as it was when the tenant moved in.

- Are the carpets clean? Hire a professional truck mount carpet cleaner. Make sure that your lease lists this as a move-out expense for the tenants. Carpet cleaning could take a few hours for cleaning and at least a day to dry. If the carpet needs to be replaced, it is best to do it before the next tenants move in or plan to do it at the next turnover. Planning means ensuring that you have the funds and time. If you have hardwood floors, do they need a professional polish? Now is the time before your new tenants' furniture is in the way.

- Is everything working properly? Ask the tenants. They may not share with you if something is not working or broken for fear that they will be charged, but ask the question. Try everything. If there are burned-out light bulbs, replace them. Have the tenants complained that the central A/C has not been keeping the place cool? In this situation, it would be important to have an HVAC person service the A/C unit.

- Remove all trash and items left by the tenants. Open every cupboard to check. Do not leave items thinking, "The next person might want it." That encourages the next tenant to leave whatever they do not want to take with them, and the whole thing snowballs into a bunch of stuff around that no one wants. The property should be completely empty except for included appliances and your welcome basket.

- Change the locks. Make sure that you have working keys and enough for you and the new tenants. Your lease should say how many keys you are to provide. I suggest changing the locks whenever you have a turnover of tenants. When you do this, you know that only you and your current tenants have access to the property. You never know if the previous tenants made copies of the keys and gave a copy to their friend or neighbor. Protect the safety and security of your investment and your tenants well being.

- Thoroughly examine appliances and other components. Check age and how well they are working. Now might be a great time to replace. No one will be inconvenienced or have food spoil because an appliance failed or a cold shower because the water heater failed. Refer to the life expectancy of housing components section of the book so you might predict how long your current appliances might last.

- Complete your annual maintenance now. That includes changing the furnace filters and batteries in smoke detectors and CO detectors. Refer to the home maintenance guide for more information. Tenant turnover is the best time for all of this work. Nothing is more frustrating for a tenant than to live in the property for a month and have the landlord call to schedule an appointment for routine maintenance. They may believe you're snooping and should have done this before they moved in.

- Find your new tenant. If you are waiting until the property is vacant and ready to rent, with everything clean and fixed, then now is the time to start advertising your rental and finding your new tenant.

- The last step in tenant turnover is to meet with your new tenants for the lease signing. Review and answer any questions that they have regarding the lease. Collect the security deposit and the rent at this time. Turn over the keys and provide the tenants with your "move-in" inspection sheet where they can document any existing damage. Review the details of the location of the mailbox, where to drop off the rent check, location and availability of parking and any other important details. Lastly, turn over the keys with a smile and welcome your tenants to their new home.

Planning ahead facilitates a smooth transition between tenants. Use the time to ensure that your rental property is in the condition you would like it to be in before your next tenant takes possession. Have a set procedure that you follow that can keep you organized and minimize how long the transition takes. Know your timeline and budget in advance. Keep in mind that every day that the property is vacant costs you money from lost rent.

Being a landlord means setting up systems to deal with tasks that get repeated time and time again. Also, you'll find many necessary decisions that will, in the end, make your rental business uniquely yours. The next section of the book is about those decisions and the many details that are a part of the process of running your rental business.

Chapter 27

Details

Details are not simply details; they are the little things that create the big picture. The details make my rental business different from yours and different from someone else's. Details are all of those little decisions that may seem simple but can have a huge impact on your rental business. So far, we have gone over the process from buying the property to setting up your business. In addition, we have covered what to do to get it rented and how to select a tenant. We have also covered details on managing things once someone is living in your rental.

Now we should look at other details. These details are the decisions that set your business apart. These details are not the how to's of the process but the personal decisions you will need to make about your business. Here we look at should I allow pets? Should I become a Section 8 landlord? Do I manage the property myself, or do I hire a property management company? These decisions can make a difference in the type of tenant you have and how much time you must spend on your rental business. They also affect your bottom line. After reading this next section, you have to decide what is important to you and what you want out of your rental business. As you read this section, you may be thinking, "What would I do in this situation," or "How do I want to handle this when it happens?" Those are good questions to consider as you read.

There is no right or wrong way. There is your way and my way, and they might be different. It is important to remember that there is no shortcut to success or an easy road to it. Being a landlord is putting in the time and taking care of all of the details, including taking the phone calls that let you know that the tenants have no heat or that they need to move out before the end of the lease. How you deal with these details is how you run your business. You are now a landlord. Let's look at what else you need to know?

Chapter 28

Tips and Tricks for Landlords

As with anything, it is the little things that make the difference. Here is a list of tips and tricks for you to keep in mind. Some you may know, and other tricks may be brand new to you. They are the details that can make a big difference in your satisfaction as a landlord.

Tips and tricks

- Photograph the property before the tenant moves in. Make sure that you have photos of any existing damage to the property that you will not be repairing before your tenant moves in. It is wise to also photograph any damage when a tenant leaves. You know the saying that a picture is worth a thousand words; that is certainly the case in this situation.
- Have professional photos taken of your rental property to use for marketing and advertising. Search for real estate photographers in your area. You can also ask your real estate agent for recommendations. Real estate photographers can offer everything from still shots to video and drone photography. You don't need to go crazy, but it is important to have good photos of your property. That does not mean shots you took with your smartphone. These photos can make the difference between getting your property rented quickly or taking a long time with few showings. Remember professional photography is easier when the property is vacant and staged, and more than likely looks its best then too.
- Test Carbon Monoxide detectors and smoke detectors. Change out the batteries when you have a change in tenants or annually. If your tenants

renew the lease, provide them with new batteries for the detectors. Carbon Monoxide detectors are not common in most properties that have not been built in the last five years. Make sure that you purchase the CO detectors and have them within fifteen feet of all bedrooms.

- Set up an online payment system for rent. Money Magazine reports that Millennials pay 61% of their bills online, and the older generations pay 42% of their bills online. Make it easy for your tenants to pay.
- Keep excellent records. Your records should include leases for five years. Receipts from money spent on the property. This record-keeping will be invaluable come tax time. Remember that money spent on repairs and improvements are tax-deductible.
- Get insurance. Not just homeowners insurance but also liability insurance. Your insurance agent who sells homeowners insurance can also write a good umbrella policy to protect you and your property. Shop around to get the best rates. You can bundle auto, home, rental and liability from the same agent saving you money and the hassle of working with multiple companies. When something goes wrong, you have one phone call to make.
- When making improvements to the property, don't buy the cheapest. If you would not put the carpet in your own home, don't put it in your rental. If it would not stand up to your careful wear and tear, do you think it will stand up to tenants? A little extra money spent on better quality will make a difference in how long the improvement lasts. The extra money spent on good quality may also mean that you can ask more for rent. Don't be a cheapskate. Don't have the mindset that the tenants will not take care of it, so I will not buy something nice. Turn that around and think, because it will be used hard, I should buy something that will withstand that hard use.
- Have a reliable handyman's phone number memorized or at the very least saved in your phone so that you can call at a moment's notice. A good handyman is a special person that can make your life as a landlord so much easier. Pay them well, and don't forget to let them know how much you appreciate them.
- Standardize the paint that you use in your rentals. Particularly when you have multiple properties knowing that they are all the same color can make a trip to the paint store and touch up a breeze. This one tip can save you both time and money. It is smart to stick with a palette of two or three colors at most, trim and body and maybe an accent. To

keep track of the information, use a Sharpie and write on the back of an outlet or switch cover the paint brand, colors, and codes.

- When considering improvements, add technology features. A smart thermostat or the Ring Video Doorbell can help your property stand out from the others that the tenant is looking to rent.
- Use a Post Office Box and keep your personal address private. Have all rent payments sent to the PO Box. You never know what lengths an unhappy tenant might go to to get your attention.
- Consider holding the title of your investment property in a Limited Liability Company (LLC) to protect your personal assets. If you decide that you want to hold your property in an LLC, you will need to establish the LLC before you write a contract to purchase the property. The contract will need to show the LLC as the buyer and not you as the individual. A good attorney can assist in establishing an LLC and educate you on the benefits and disadvantages of holding a property in an LLC.

Now you have some tricks you can use to run your rental business. Now let's look at some other details.

Chapter 29

Hire a Property Manager or Self-Manage My Property?

Answering this question may not be as easy as you think. It may require you to do some soul searching and a review of your life to see if managing a rental property is right for you. Be sure to consider the pros and cons of your situation before you decide. Look at your rental properties, career goals and personal priorities. What are the nuts and bolts of managing your rental property? Let's first take a look at the tasks involved in managing a rental.

The tasks involved in managing your property include
- Preparing the lease
- Determining the rental rate to be charged
- Advertising the property
- Tenant screening
- Collecting the rent
- Routine maintenance
- Making repairs
- Fielding complaints
- Moderating issues between tenants
- Checking in with tenants and the property once a quarter
- Enforcing the lease
- Evicting the tenant if necessary
- Filling a vacancy when it occurs

This is a long list of responsibilities. Deciding whether you can or want to do this yourself versus hiring a management company is an important decision. Self-management will certainly save you money. However, a property management company can execute the above list quickly and professionally, but they typically charge anywhere between seven to eleven percent of the monthly rent. They also charge for repair expenses and replacement items—that is, the cost of the item requiring repair and the cost of the maintenance person to do the work or supervision of the work being completed by another professional. Hiring a property management company means that you step back and let the management company handle everything from A to Z—advertising, rent collection, maintenance, and the rest of the above list.

If you decide that you will self-manage, you are not only the landlord but also the person responsible for the day-to-day operations and keeping the property up to date and in good repair. You will be your tenants' only contact for everything. Self-management has its advantages if you have the time and the skills necessary to do it well. Yet there are also many disadvantages. Let's take a look at the pros and cons of self-management.

Pros of self-management
- **Greater control:** Self-management means that you take care of everything yourself. You are the person making the decisions regarding your property, and you know what is going on. Some people are just more comfortable being in control of the details and have trouble delegating. If you are that person, then self-management may be perfect for you.
- **Closer relationship with tenants:** If you are the tenants' point of contact, you can develop a closer relationship with them. Of course, landlord/tenant relationships are not always sweet, which means that this is not always a benefit. At those times, you may wish that you had someone else involved.
- **Financial savings:** This alone can be the determining factor because self-management can save you from seven to eleven percent of each month's rent. So, if you are charging $1,000 a month in rent, you save between $70 and $110 each month. You can also save on maintenance provided by the in-house crews used by property management companies. Those crews often cost more than what contractors would

cost to do the same job. If you are a handy person and do some of the required repairs yourself, that can mean an even greater savings to you!

- **Experience:** When you manage your own property, you will be learning on the job. That on-the-job experience can mean that you have some hiccups along the way, but those can be great ways to learn. Some landlords decide that they enjoy the property management portion of this process so much that they may wish to focus on property management as a career. That is a big step, but you can keep property management as your side job if you love it.

Cons of self-management

- **Time required:** If that list of responsibilities provided above looks overwhelming, that is because it can be. Remember that is required for each property that you own. The time that it takes to care for your property and complete those tasks can be significant. This could be enough of a reason to hire a property management company.
- **Lack of experience:** If you are just starting out as a landlord, you will encounter situations that you simply have no experience with. You do not know best practices or legal regulations. It can take a long time to gain the experience and expertise necessary to manage a property well without running into problems.
- **Setting rent too high or too low:** This is another situation where experience can teach you how to research to arrive at the right price for the property. Without that experience, you may set the price too low and miss out on income or too high and miss out on good potential tenants. A property management company knows the local rental rates and can aid you in finding the right amount to charge, given the location of the property and the amenities. This could mean more money in your pocket every month.
- **Source of stress:** Taking on all of the responsibilities of managing your property can certainly cause stress. If a tenant has a burst pipe in the middle of the night, you will be the person that takes the call and needs to get the situation resolved as soon as possible. If a tenant is not following the regulations as a part of the lease, you are the person that has to confront them. You have to follow up to ensure that the situation has been resolved or address the consequences.

So we have reviewed the pros and cons of self-management. Let's review the pros and cons of property management. There are certainly some great reasons to choose a property management company over self-management.

Pros of property management

- **More time:** Probably the biggest reason to choose a property management company is the time savings for you. You won't receive phone calls from the tenants regarding a maintenance problem, and you won't need to worry about traveling and not being available to a tenant. Additionally, you do not have to worry about the impact on your family time because of the rental.
- **Built-in maintenance staff:** Someone else will be handing your property and day-to-day operations of your rental. You won't have to worry about finding a fair quote for work to be done or be left trying to find a contractor with the availability that you need. The property management company has you taken care of.
- **The property manager's experience:** One of the big advantages you gain with a property manager is their valuable knowledge gained from years of experience. They have experience dealing with issues and problems. They have seen things before and know how to deal with them. They know the best way to handle most situations. They have an office full of people, and if they have not had the experience, someone else in the office has and knows just what to do.
- **The property manager's expertise:** When it comes to best practices, rules, and regulations, relying on a property manager can give you peace of mind. Property managers are committed to understanding rental law and state statutes that they must abide by.
- **Prompt filling of vacancies:** Property management companies have the resources available to find quality tenants. They have the screening processes in place and know how to avoid Fair Housing issues.
- **Property managers manage the finances:** They collect the money, pay the bills, and provide you with a monthly income statement. Depending on how well you keep records, this can be a huge win, particularly at tax time.

Cons of property management

- **The cost:** Remember that property management companies typically charge between seven to eleven percent of the rent, plus expenses for managing your property. This is the method that most companies figure their fees on. Some companies may charge differently. Make sure you know the costs involved and how you will be charged.

- **The management company may have a tenant screening process that is too strict or too relaxed:** Your property manager must follow state landlord law to the letter, but you may find some wiggle room when you are screening for a new tenant. The property manager does not have that ability. This means that it may take the management company longer to find you a tenant, or they may pass on tenants that you would have approved.
- **You have no opportunity to gain experience:** When you have a property management company managing your property, you never gain the experience, which may mean that you might one day be able to manage the property for yourself. Depending on your goals, distancing yourself from daily operations could certainly be a disadvantage.
- **Property managers that disappoint:** Plenty of property managers are not worth their fees. They can fail to deliver on the advantages that you expected. If they are not running things the way you expected, that in itself becomes a stress. Be sure to be cautious, interviewing multiple managers before you make your selection.
- **You have less control over your property:** You have everything done for you, so you do not have a hand in the tenant selection, setting the price or the maintenance and upkeep of your property.
- **Maintenance provided by the in-house crews may cost more than what contractors would charge:** The work provided by the in-house maintenance may be more expensive and not be up to your quality standards.

Using a property management company can remove much stress from your life. It can mean that you have time to do what you really want to do, rather than managing your rental property. The bottom line is the decision is yours and should be well thought through before being made. How do tenants feel about properties managed by an individual landlord versus a property management company? Let's look at that before you make your final decision.

Chapter 30

Do Tenants Prefer Property Managers or Owners As Landlords?

How will the experience be different for your tenants if you use a property management company? Tenants value the ability to contact someone who will take care of their needs promptly. If a tenant experiences a maintenance issue, they want their problem solved quickly. If you are a landlord who always carries your phone with you and answers when someone calls, your tenant will promptly get the attention they need.

A property management company can provide that same service. Someone is available to answer the phone during business hours. But in addition to having the phone answered, your tenant expects a quick resolution to their problem. You, as the landlord, want a quick resolution and repair. The broken pipe or the leaky toilet is causing damage to your investment. The longer the issue goes on, the worse the situation can get.

What is the property management company's policy for after-hours phone calls? Do they have a number that the tenant can call in the middle of the night for a maintenance problem? Know that tenants who have had a poor experience with a property management company will likely remember that experience and may shy away from properties not managed by individual owners. Those potential tenants appreciate the personal touch they get from properties managed by owners. Often they feel that the owner-managed property is in better overall condition and maintained better.

Tenants care about the efficiency of the rental experience. Do you provide the ability for easy payment of rent? Can the tenant pay online from their account to yours?

Remember that you want your tenants to have a great experience renting from you. The more positive their experience, the more likely they will stay long-term. A long-term tenant saves you time and money. A happy, long-term tenant can also refer their friends to you and, more than likely, be much like them and great tenants that you want to have.

So the question remains. Should I hire a property manager or do it myself? In order to decide if you would be better off self-managing or using a property management company, you should consider the pros and cons and your own personal situation. Here are some questions to ask yourself in order to help you determine which option is best for you.

Questions to consider before making your decision
- How many rental properties do I own? Does that number make self-management an option for me?
- Do I live in close proximity to the properties that I own?
- Would the time investment keep me from my other career or personal goals?
- Do I desire to keep work time and personal time separate?
- Do I have the experience and/or expertise necessary to carry out the responsibilities of being a landlord? Am I willing to learn and take the bumps along the way while I learn?

Whatever you decide, know that you can make a change if what you are doing is not working. Perhaps after having a property management company manage your properties for a while, you feel that you have gained the knowledge to do it yourself. Try it. But, on the other hand, after managing your properties for a while, you may decide that it is not worth the time commitment and the stress. Hire a management company. Perhaps you have multiple properties, and you would like to try just managing one to start with. Select the one that you live closest to and try it!

After several months it will be important to re-evaluate. Ask yourself some questions. How does it feel to manage my own property? Do I feel overwhelmed? Do I feel like I have the knowledge to look out for my own best interest? Am I frustrated with the time commitment? Once you have the honest answers to these questions, you will know whether you should use a property management company or manage your property yourself. The decision is not final. You can re-evaluate whenever you feel your personal situation has changed. Your job may change, and it may require travel. You may have a new baby in the family. These might be good reasons to consider using a property management company. Perhaps your time instead has been freed up by retirement, and you feel like you could self-manage.

If you have decided that you would like to use a property management company to handle your rentals, how do you decide which one you should hire? What is important to look for in a property management company? In the next chapter, we will answer these questions.

Chapter 31

How Do I Choose a Property Management Company?

Choosing the right property management company can make all of the difference in your rental business. Getting the right one can help you realize all of the potential benefits. Know that not all management companies are the same. Talk to several companies before you make your decision. Remember that you will be partnering with this person and the company to manage your properties. It is important to have a rapport with the person.

Here are some questions to ask when meeting with a property manager

- What is your experience in property management?
- How will you market the property?
- How quickly do you typically get tenants for available properties?
- What is your process for screening tenants?
- How do you handle maintenance requests?
- Do you provide maintenance services?
- How do you handle late or lack of payment of rent?
- If eviction is required, how is it handled?
- What are your fees? Remember, cheapest is not always best, and you often do get what you pay for.

Please do not decide on your property management company by fees alone. Fees are a valid consideration. However, often choosing the company that charges the least means you may also receive the least service.

It will also be important to ask the property management company to provide you with references. Remember that you do not want just anyone managing your properties. Your reputation as a landlord will be tied, at least in part, to the performance of your management company. Make sure that the values of the company mirror your values. You want your tenants treated with respect and to know that they are valued. When your management company reflects your values, is experienced, and provides pleasant interactions with you and your tenants, it is far easier for you to take a more hands-off approach. Now you can enjoy the experience of someone else taking care of your investment.

Even with someone else managing your rental, there are still detailed decisions that you must make about your rental. One big one is whether you will allow tenants to have pets. Let's look at that question in greater detail.

Chapter 32

Pets or No Pets?

One of the decisions to make as a landlord is whether or not you will allow pets, and your answer affects your rental and you as a landlord dramatically. As you sort out this decision for yourself, what are the advantages and disadvantages? How do you operate your rental business based on pets or no pet policy?

The list of advantages can be rather short as to why you should allow pets. The best reason to allow pets is to increase the pool of tenants you can rent to. Another advantage is that you can charge higher rent. This can be in the form of more rent charged per month, a pet rental fee that is charged each month, or you may decide to charge a non-refundable pet deposit. With a pet deposit, part of the deposit can be non-refundable, and the rest of the pet deposit is refundable if there is no damage. This can motivate the tenant to more closely monitor their pet so that they do not cause damage to the property.

The disadvantages list is also short. The major disadvantage is that pets can cause damage. Notice I said that they *can* cause damage. They may not. However, cats and dogs have hair and hair left behind can be considered, by some, to be damage. If you rent to someone who has a pet, it is difficult to rent to someone with a pet allergy after that. The flooring would have to be replaced, air ducts cleaned, and the property might need painting to ensure that an allergic person would not have a reaction. Also, it goes without saying that the property would require a very deep cleaning once the tenant and pet leave.

Some landlords decide to allow cats but not dogs; others decide that dogs are fine, but cats are not. Cats are small and do not typically scratch woodwork and floors, but they can spray. The spraying can cause significant damage requiring the replacement of flooring and possible repainting. The spraying cannot necessarily be predicted or controlled by the tenant.

Though puppies may seem sweet, damage caused by dogs may include scratching woodwork, doors, and floors. They may also urinate on the floors. Young or lonely dogs may chew anything they can get their mouths on. Outside they can cause damage to yards, killing grass or digging holes.

After reading this, you may wonder why you would ever allow pets. This is a decision that you must make. If you decide that you will allow a pet, it is wise to approve each individual pet. Meet the pet and see how it behaves and how the owner interacts with the animal. Note that you should check with your homeowners' insurance and see if they have restrictions regarding animals on your policy. Some insurance companies restrict specific dog breeds. You do not want a tenant moving in with a restricted breed and then have something happen. In that case, your homeowners' insurance would not cover you if you became involved in a lawsuit.

Another thing to check is HOA documents if your property is within an HOA. They may have restrictions regarding breed, how many animals, and the type of animal allowed. Some HOA's do not allow tenants to have pets at all.

You could decide that you might allow pets just this once. You have worn, tired carpet, and you plan to replace it when this next tenant leaves. Or, you have a great applicant who has a cat, and you don't want to reject the tenant's application solely because of the cat. Remember that once you have had a pet on the property, a future tenant sensitive to pets may not be able to rent from you because of the pet dander that is difficult to completely remove from the property. The cat may spray and require that you paint in addition to replacing the carpet. Is it worth what might happen? Remember to keep the big picture in mind and always be patient!

We have talked about dogs and cats, but tenants can have reptiles, fish, and other furry animals that live in cages like rabbits, guinea pigs, hamsters, gerbils, and ferrets. If you allow pets make sure you know all of the animals that your tenant will be moving into your property. Weigh the advantages and disadvantages and decide if tenants with pets are right for you.

Some say it is easier to allow pets and deal with the aftermath when the tenant moves out. When you allow pets, you have more potential tenants to choose from. If you screen the potential tenant carefully, you may be able to make some additional money. Not all pet owners are irresponsible, and not all pets cause damage. Whether or not to allow pets should be considered carefully, weighing the advantages and disadvantages.

You may decide not to allow pets and then find out that your tenant has one anyway. It can be disturbing when you are called to make a repair, you arrive at your rental, and you see a cat sitting in the window. Make sure that your lease covers what to do in this situation.

A pet is a pet, right? Not necessarily. What about service animals? What about emotional support animals? The next chapter will provide you with important information that you need to know about these animals.

Chapter 33

Service Animals and Emotional Support Animals

As a landlord, you will more than likely encounter the issue of service animals or emotional support animals at some point. What do you do when a prospective tenant tells you that they have a service animal or an emotional support animal, and you have decided that you do not want pets in your rental?

Federal laws, and often, state laws, are in place regarding service and emotional support animals. The law requires that landlords provide accommodations for both service animals and emotional support animals. In general, a tenant has the right to a service animal or emotional support animal even if the rental does not allow pets. As the landlord in this situation, you are not allowed to charge a pet deposit or an extra pet rental for the qualified service animal. The tenant is liable for damage that the animal causes. However, you do have the right to reject an aggressive animal or if a tenant cannot provide the necessary documentation of their need for the animal. But if the animal is not aggressive and you are provided with the necessary paperwork, you must allow the animal. Remember that this animal is not legally considered a pet.

So what is an emotional support animal (ESA)? An emotional support animal can be anything from a dog, cat, ferret, fish, pig, bird, turtle or anything else that the qualifying owner wants. Wild or exotic animals do not qualify under the emotional support guidelines. If the animal is not a domesticated species or is considered dangerous, they would not count as support animals. The animal's purpose is to comfort the owner. They typically do not perform tasks, but instead, they provide comfort and make the human feel better. People with diagnosed disorders or disabilities may get an ESA. Examples of these disorders may include anxiety, depression, and learning disabilities. How does someone obtain an ESA? A licensed mental health professional such as a therapist, psychiatrist, or psychologist must write an official letter of permission. A patient is prescribed a support animal as a part of the patient's treatment plan. The professional decides whether the patient would benefit from an ESA. Not all people with depression, for example, have ESA. An emotional support animal is legally considered to assist a person with a disability. This is much like a service animal assisting someone with a physical disability.

A service animal is not the same as an emotional support animal. There are distinct differences. Service animals are dogs as opposed to ESAs, which can be any type of animal. These dogs are trained to perform work that the disabled person cannot do or assist the person with their disability.

Below are some examples of tasks performed by a service dog
- Opening doors
- Answering when the phone rings
- Reminding person to take medication
- Guiding a person with visual impairments
- Detecting a seizure before it happens
- Picking up dropped items or performing other basic tasks

A service animal must be allowed if the prospective tenant meets certain qualifications.

Required qualifications
- The tenant has a real, recognized disability
- The animal assists with the person's ability to cope with the disability

As the landlord, you have the right to verify the prospective tenant's disability. If the disability is not obvious, you can ask for a doctor's note confirming that the patient has a disability and benefits from having a service animal. It is okay to make sure that your prospective tenant has the proper approvals and paperwork. As with an emotional support animal, you may not charge a pet deposit for a service animal. The disabled person must be able to rent the property without paying any additional fees for the animal. A service animal is not considered a pet; they help disabled people have equal access to housing and a better quality of life.

This said, in some cases, you may legally reject a service animal. If the dog poses an unreasonable risk of physically harming others or there is a high likelihood of property damage. The risk must be obvious. What if the prospective tenant wants to get a second dog. The first one is an ESA animal. Can you say no to the second dog? Yes, if the second dog is not an ESA animal, you can say no!

A Helpful Hint! A service or emotional support animal is not considered a pet and may not be rejected if you are provided with proper paperwork and proof of disability. You may not charge a pet deposit or pet rent.

A person with a service animal or an emotional support animal must still meet all of your requirements for a prospective tenant. For example, they must meet minimum credit scores and minimum income requirements, credit history and whatever you have set up as your screening guidelines. If the prospective tenant meets or exceeds your requirements, you may not reject the person due to the service or emotional support animal. If you do, you may be opening yourself to legal action for housing discrimination.

If you have been a landlord for any length of time, you will have received a phone call or two from people asking if you accept Section 8. The next chapter will cover what Section 8 is and how you can become a Section 8 landlord if you choose.

Chapter 34

Section 8—What Is It and Do I Have to Participate?

If you own or plan to purchase a property that will be used as a rental property, you will need to decide whether you want to become a Section 8 landlord. What is Section 8? Section 8 was established by the Federal Government in the 1970s to provide housing assistance to those in financial need rather than offering public housing. This is because it was decided that it was easier and less expensive for the federal government to offer housing assistance instead of building and managing low-income housing. Renters that qualify for Section 8 make less than fifty percent of the median income in a given area. The potential renter that qualifies and participates in the Section 8 program receives a rental voucher that will cover up to seventy percent of the rent each month. The renter will cover the other thirty percent of the rent. The voucher is paid directly to the participating landlord each month.

Section 8 vouchers do not grant Section 8 tenants access to every rental unit in a community. The rental and landlord must both participate in the Section 8 program in order for the tenant to be able to rent a specific property. The rental property must meet specific requirements. The approved housing must have a certain number of bedrooms and bathrooms, and only a certain amount can be charged in rent for the property. If you are a landlord participating in Section 8 and the public housing authority believes you are asking for more than the market rent on your property, you may be required to reduce your rental rate to continue to participate in the program.

If you decide that you are interested in being a Section 8 landlord, you must take certain steps to be approved. First, you must make an application with the local public housing authority and fill out all required paperwork. Before making an application, ensure that your property matches the requirements and qualities required by the Housing Authority. Once your personal application is approved, your property must also pass an inspection. For as long as you participate in the program, the inspection will be repeated annually. When your property is inspected, you'll need to show a working kitchen, bathrooms, and overall indicators that the property is well maintained. The inspector will also look for chipped paint and plumbing or electrical code violations. Of course, you must have heating and perhaps cooling units for your property. Next, your lease must be submitted to the Housing Authority, and it must also be approved. Once the paperwork is in, the inspection is acceptable, the lease is approved, and the rental rate is agreed upon, then you and your rental are approved for the Section 8 program.

Now that you have completed the approval process, your next step will be to find qualified tenants and screen them just like you would if you were not participating in the Section 8 program. The participants in the program must meet certain standards to qualify for the program, but it is still wise as the landlord to conduct your own screening, including background check and verification of income. Note that to be approved to participate in the program and receive Section 8 benefits, the prospective tenant must pass a credit check and often a background check.

What are the advantages and disadvantages of participating in the program?

Advantages include:
- Free advertising—often including a free website through your local public housing authority
- Reduced vacancy rates for your rental—when a vacancy does occur it can often be filled quickly
- You are guaranteed an income
- Your tenants are partially screened
- Seventy percent of the rent is paid directly to you and is guaranteed

The disadvantages include:
- Your property must submit to yearly inspections

- Rental price caps—the HUD determines your maximum allowable rental rate. For example, if HUD determines that the maximum rent on a three-bedroom condo is $1400, you may not charge more even if the current market rate in the area of your rental is higher.
- Many landlords feel that participation in Section 8 means that they have a lower quality tenant. They feel that by accepting a Section 8 tenant, they open themselves up to the possibility of tenants having problems with job stability, a greater likelihood of property damage, and a greater chance of dealing with evictions. Often these potential problems can be avoided by detailed tenant screening.

A Helpful Hint! If you decide to raise your rent while you and your property are a part of the Section 8 program, you must get approval from the public housing authority.

Deciding whether to become a Section 8 landlord is a personal choice. In most areas, landlords are not required to accept Section 8 tenants. The only way to be sure that you are not required to participate is to check with your local and state laws. Specific information regarding HUD rules can be found on their website. As a landlord, you may feel that the disadvantages outweigh the advantages of participating in the Section 8 program.

The next chapter covers a topic that you could have dealt with if you have been a landlord for any length of time. If you have not dealt with this situation, it will more than likely come up. Do you handle it the same way that I suggest?

Chapter 35

My Tenant Wants to Break the Lease

So you just received a phone call or text, and your tenant tells you that they need to move. Life happens. Perhaps you have been in this situation. When you least expect it, maybe when you were not even looking, you get a great job offer that requires that you move. Then again, the phone call or text may be letting you know that your tenant's mom is dying and she needs help in her final months. Remember those moments? What do you do as the landlord of this tenant?

Remember that life happens; this is what you can do. Remind your tenant that they are indeed responsible for the rent until the end of the lease *or* until you can get the property rented to someone else. Make every effort to get the place rented as soon as possible. Let the tenant know that you will expect their utmost cooperation to get this done. That may mean short notice showings or showings on the property at less than ideal times. Let them know that you expect them to make sure that the property always looks its best so that you can get it rented quickly. Perhaps you can rent the property for more money than the current tenant pays. That would be a win for both you and the tenant.

Sometimes being a landlord is about being human and compassionate. With the examples that I have presented, I would react in a caring manner. But what if you receive a phone call or text and the tenant tells you they are not getting along with their roommate and they want out of the lease yet are willing to pay for the rest of their part of the lease? In this situation, I would have many questions. What exactly is going on between the roommates? Why is it that you feel that you can no longer live together? Do you feel unsafe, or is it that they are just not cleaning up after themselves? Have you talked to your roommate about the situation? What was their reaction? Did anything change?

They've answered your questions; now what? You could mediate the situation and sit down with the two roommates to see if you can get their relationship to a better place. If things remain ugly, then what? Is it time to find new tenants, or are you better off making them stick it out? Is this a life lesson for the tenant that they need to be careful about who they enter into a lease with? Perhaps. If you let one roommate out of the lease by allowing them to pay for the rest of the lease, what happens to the tenant that is left having to pay their portion of the rent and full utilities? You may also decide to do nothing and let the tenants work out the situation for themselves. If you decide to do nothing, make sure that the situation is safe for all parties. Sometimes doing nothing allows the situation to resolve itself.

In any situation, it is a good idea not to react. The tenants need someone to provide them with a well-thought-out answer to their questions. Take a deep breath before you answer. You can always say, "Let me get back to you." Buy yourself some time to explore what is best, given the situation.

After your experience with your tenants, you have decided that you do not want to renew the lease with them. What do you do? That topic is covered in the next chapter.

Chapter 36

I Want My Tenants to Leave at the End of the Lease

It is getting close to the end of the lease, and you do not want to renew the lease with your tenant! Now, what do you do? You will need to write a "notice to vacate letter" to your tenant. It will be crucial to do everything by the book. It might be wise to consult the attorney you work with for specifics and guidance. Once you have written a "notice to vacate letter", you may keep the template on file and use it as needed in the future. This section will just go over the basics of what to do.

If you will not be renewing the lease with your tenant, it is important to give the tenant as much notice as possible, and the best way to do so is with a letter. The letter should be provided as soon as sixty days before the end of the lease and at a minimum of thirty days. If you have a month-to-month lease with the tenant, proper notice must be received by the tenant at least ten days before the last day of the rental month. The lease that your tenant signed may give you details as to exactly when the tenant must be notified. Follow the specifics in the lease. Be aware of any state laws that may come into play in this situation. The more time you give your tenant, the more time you will have to work out any problems.

When putting together a lease termination or "notice to vacate letter", you will always need to include the following information:
- The property address
- The tenancy period

- The landlord's name and contact information—this is included so the tenant can contact you with any questions
- Tenant's names and contact information
- What date the move-out will occur
- When the property inspection will occur
- What happens with the tenant's security deposit

Other details to consider while writing this letter include, are you within your legal rights to ask your tenant to leave, and what are you asking the tenant to do. Be very clear. How much time does the tenant have to respond to the notice? Can the tenant make amends, or are they required to move out? As long as your letter covers all of these questions clearly, contains the above information, and does not break any state or local laws, you have a successfully written "notice to vacate letter".

You may include information regarding why you are not renewing the lease. For example, you are selling the property or if the tenant broke the lease terms. Be as clear as possible. However, if the tenant has just driven you crazy or been difficult to deal with, keep that information to yourself.

You may consider sending the tenant an email rather than a formal letter; not a good idea. The tenant needs to receive the notice by mail, for this is how legal documents are processed. It is wise to have the post office send a certified letter with a "return receipt requested" so that you have knowledge and proof that the tenant received the letter.

What happens next? In most cases, the tenant will follow through with the request and move out by the prescribed date. They may have questions or concerns after the letter. Typically you and the tenant can work out any problems during the move-out process. In some cases, the tenant may disagree with the request or simply refuse to move out. This is when you will need to consult an attorney, and you will need to begin the eviction process.

If you have not ever written one of these letters, it can feel a bit overwhelming. Make sure you are within your rights to serve the tenant with the letter. Send the notice within the appropriate amount of time and follow the guidelines above to write the letter. Carefully following these steps will ensure that you are doing the right thing as a landlord.

The best way of learning about anything is by doing.

–Richard Branson

Chapter 37

Does Time of Year Affect Renting My Property?

Does it make a difference if you try to rent your property in July or November? Does it matter to you what time of year you move? Most people prefer to move during May, June, or July. During these months, you have the best chances for good weather, and if you have children, moving during these months least disrupts the school year. This means the time of year can affect you greatly as a landlord.

A property available for rent in November has a smaller pool of tenants looking to rent, which may cause delays in finding an excellent tenant and the potential for a longer vacancy. If you look at the numbers, what does that mean to you? Let's say that the last time you rented your place was in July. You were able to charge $1,400 a month. Your tenant moved out, and now you are trying to get your place rented, and it is November. You have had one call, and it has been advertised for almost two weeks. What do you do? Lower the amount that you are asking. If you lower the amount to $1,300, you will not earn as much; in fact, you will be down $1,200 for the year. However, if you have the property vacant for a month, you will have your income on the property down by $1,300. You are better off charging less per month than having the property vacant for a month. Round numbers are used for this example, but remember, $1,295 is so much less psychologically than $1,300.

The best time to rent a property in Northern Colorado is with a lease period from August 1st to July 31st. This is the schedule followed by most property management companies. Individual owners have found that it works well for them to follow a similar schedule when possible. If you lease your property based on that schedule, you have the largest pool of potential tenants. When this is the case, you have the likelihood of being able to charge the highest amount in rent. Following the idea of supply and demand, when you have greater demand, you can charge more and have more tenants to choose from.

A Helpful Hint! When you fill out your lease, in addition to putting dates for the start and end of the lease period, put a time that the lease ends—for example, 7/31/2025 at 1:00 pm MST. Some property management companies have the lease end two days before the end of the month. That is great for the management company or you, the landlord, but that can leave the tenant with nowhere to go for two days. This is something to consider.

If you have a tenant move out before the end of the lease period, it is a good idea to offer a shorter lease period to the new tenant so that you more closely match the August to July schedule. It is not a good idea to be renting a place in December and offer a one-year lease. If you offer six- or seven-month leases, at the end of the lease period, you will have a larger pool of prospective tenants to choose from and, therefore, may be able to charge more for rent. You can offer a one-year lease at the end of the short-term lease.

If I have to fill a vacancy outside of May, June, or July, I like to let prospective tenants know that I am offering a short lease, but the lease will renew annually after that. I have had tenants say that they would like to sign a nineteen-month lease in that situation. Remember that your tenant benefits most from the long lease. They know that the rental rate charged will not change, and they do not have to move. If you are very comfortable with the tenant and believe that they will be great to have around for that long, go ahead and do the long-term lease. If you have any concerns, opt not to do the longer lease.

You are learning how to handle the details of running your rental business. What do you know about maintaining your property? The next chapter will educate you about the maintenance and upkeep of your property. You have your handyman's phone number saved in your phone, but there is more to know than that. Read on!

Chapter 38

How Do I Maintain My Rental Property?

You now own another property, and you are responsible for the upkeep and maintenance of that property. You want to protect and take care of your investment. What should you know? A rule of thumb can help guide you when budgeting for repairs. According to a popular guide, the one percent rule, you should set aside at least one percent of your property value for home maintenance each year. For example, according to this guideline, if your property is worth $375,000, you should be spending $3,750 per year or about $312 per month. Some years you could spend more, some years you could spend less. It is impossible to predict how much maintenance your rental property will need. It is also difficult to know how much it will cost and when that maintenance will become necessary. The one percent rule is only a rough estimate.

Another practical estimate for maintenance costs is the square foot rule. This rule is to budget $1 per square foot annually for maintenance. This guide takes into account that the larger the property, the more money will need to be spent on maintaining the property. Neither of these guides considers market prices for contractors and building materials. Both materials and contractors' rates can vary dramatically from region to region of the country.

Here are some factors to consider when budgeting for the maintenance of your property. How much you may need to spend depends on the property you purchase. A property built in the last ten years will likely need very little maintenance. The older the home, the more likely it will need maintenance and repairs. Additionally, the previous owners' maintenance, or lack thereof, will affect the care required and the maintenance budget for your ownership of the property.

Every component within the home has a life to it. Your kitchen appliances have an expected length of time that they will last. Water heaters have an expected life. So do furnaces, roofs, plumbing, and electrical. National Home Builders have completed a study on the life expectancy of home components. Some of those findings will be on the chart located in this chapter. It is possible to purchase a well-maintained twenty-year-old home that has been prepared well for sale that will provide you with trouble-free home ownership for years to come.

Part of owning a rental property is providing your tenant with a safe and livable home. It is common sense, but also the law. Make sure that you know your local and state laws regarding health and safety codes for rentals. In general, most health and safety codes require minimum standards for the cleanliness of a property. There are also typical requirements regarding working plumbing and water supplies. Other housing and safety codes set electrical wiring, HVAC equipment, and fire prevention standards. Security is also included in habitability. You, as a landlord, should make sure that your rental meets the requirements for safety and habitability. You should care for your investment property in much the same way as you would care for your own home.

I do not believe that any of us set out to maintain our properties in a manner that would require the city, county, or state to get involved regarding the health, safety, and maintenance of the property. Maintaining a property is a shared responsibility of both the landlord and the tenant. As the owner of a rental, make sure to have clear steps to follow regarding repair and maintenance issues when they arise. Do you have a form that you want to be completed? Do you want to be notified by phone, email, or text? Make sure that your tenants are aware of their maintenance responsibilities, which are outlined in the lease. If you are not notified of a necessary repair, the tenant could be considered in neglect of the property. Have the right attitude about repairs and calls from tenants about maintenance that needs to be done. Remember that the tenant is helping you protect your investment and helping you care for the property when you are notified of repairs being needed. Answer the tenant's request promptly and with a smile.

Twice a year, provide tenants with a checklist so they can report any issues with the property. Remind them that you are interested in safety concerns, hazards, and maintenance problems. This form can be emailed with a request that the form be returned. Respond promptly to the information received from the tenant. Also, use a written tenant checklist when tenants move out. In addition to the tenant checklist, thoroughly inspect your property before new tenants move in. When you have a tenant renewing their lease, make sure that you do another inspection and have any necessary repairs completed promptly.

Don't assume that your tenants know how to handle maintenance problems. It is important to show them some basics of home care, such as how to change a furnace filter and what to do when a circuit breaker is tripped. It is also wise to show them how to restart a tripped garbage disposal. Beyond that, I would not advise that you have your tenants do repairs. Provide tenants with a list of maintenance dos and don'ts. Request that the tenant notify you immediately regarding plumbing, heating, or security problems.

It is wise to keep a written log of all complaints and requests for repairs. Also include when the complaint was remedied, the cost of repair, and the service provider. If there are problems in the future, you can easily call back the service provider that did the work.

What basic home maintenance tasks should be completed regularly to keep your rental in top shape? Regularly completed general maintenance helps you get the maximum life out of your properties' components.

Basic home maintenance includes checking the following annually

- Check grout and caulking—touch up voids to protect against water damage
- Check for plumbing leaks under sinks, around toilets and in showers
- Check the sump pump
- Do a visual inspection of the water heater
- Test smoke and carbon monoxide detectors—replace batteries
- Have HVAC systems cleaned and serviced
- Provide tenants with furnace filters and verify that the filters are being replaced regularly—a minimum of once every three months
- Walk around the property's exterior—trim vegetation if needed, test the lawn sprinkler system for leaks, and ensure the sprinkler system has winterization blowouts done.

- In the fall, call tenants before the first freezing temperature to ensure that hoses are disconnected from hose bibs
- Before bitter cold temperatures, have tenants leave doors to cabinets open so pipes don't freeze
- Clean out the gutters and check for leaks

A Helpful Hint! An experience that I had when I was a renter that always makes me smile dates back to when my husband and I first moved to Fort Collins, CO. We rented a duplex on West Mountain. We paid our rent on time and typically never heard from the property owner. During the first fall that we lived in the duplex, on the night of the first predicted freezing temperatures, we received a phone call from the landlord. He asked that we go out and check to make sure that all of the hoses were disconnected from the hose bibs. We did. The next fall, we received the same phone call. That happened every year of the four years that we lived there. Fast forward several years to the first fall in our home. We did not receive that phone call because we were homeowners. Guess what? We forgot to check and did not disconnect one hose. The pipe froze and broke, and we had a small flood in the basement. As much as I laughed every year that we received that phone call from our landlord to remind us to disconnect hoses, I now wished it still had occurred, even though I was now a homeowner. So plan on making that phone call every fall if your rental has exterior hose bibs. That one call can save you money, time, and prevent damage.

Home maintenance every two to five years
- Fireplaces should be serviced. Clean gas log fireplaces every couple of years, depending on use. For wood-burning fireplaces, clean the chimney every couple of years, depending on use.
- Clean clothes dryer exhaust vents.
- Replace caulking around windows and doors.

Home maintenance every five to ten years
- Paint the exterior of the property.
- Budget and plan on replacing the dishwasher.
- Replace the microwave. Small countertop microwaves typically will not last five to ten years, but built-in models will wear out after about nine years of use.

Home maintenance every ten to fifteen years
- Plan on replacing the water heater in this time frame.
- Replace the garage door opener.
- Replace smoke and carbon monoxide detectors.

Home maintenance every fifteen-plus years

Reaching this point in home maintenance means that you have gone full circle. You have replaced everything, and you are starting over again. Some items on this list have big price tags, and the replacement of these items may require some planning and saving for.

- Replace the roof, depending on the roofing material and the climate. Replacing the roof can need to occur anytime between twenty and forty years.
- Budget for replacement of HVAC systems, including furnace and central A/C units. Properly servicing these units can add length to the life of the equipment, but plan on replacing them between fifteen and twenty years.
- If your rental has a deck, plan on replacement. Decking materials have greatly improved in recent years with the introduction of Trex and other composite decking materials. You do not have to choose wood. Do your research and select replacement products that will function well and give the new deck a long life. Your choice should also take into account the climate where your property is located.
- Replace bathroom and kitchen faucets and sinks—this is a task that could be performed by you or a handyman. Remember to select quality. It will save you money over the long term.

This checklist provides you with a plan for home maintenance. The better you maintain your rental, the longer the components will last, and the better price you may get for your property when it comes time to sell. Buyers can certainly tell the difference between a property that has been taken care of and maintained well and one that has not been. Renters also appreciate a well-maintained property. Maintaining your property communicates that you care about it. Consider time and money spent on maintenance as protecting your investment.

Life Expectancy of Housing Components

Home Component	Life Expectancy in Years
Refrigerator	13 years
Dishwasher	9 years
Electric Range	13 years
Gas Range	15 years
Clothes Washer	10 years

Clothes Dryer	13 years
Central A/C	15 years
Water Heater (Gas)	10 years
Water Heater (Electric)	11 years
Furnace (Gas)	18 years
Carpet	8 years
Garage Door Opener	13 years
Roof	20 years
Sprinkler/Irrigation Controls	15 years

(National Home Builders Association Study of Life Expectancy of Home Components 2007)

The actual life expectancy of the components of a home depends on several factors. Those factors include the level of maintenance, climate conditions, and the intensity of use. The conclusion could be drawn that the components in a rental property may have heavier use and, therefore, a shorter life. This table is a general guideline only and is not a warranty or guarantee regarding the life expectancy of any particular product.

Most repairs can be made to your rental with minimal disruption to your tenants. But what are you supposed to do when something major happens? How to handle this situation will be discussed in the next chapter.

Chapter 39

What Do I Do If My Rental Needs Extensive Repairs?

As a landlord, you have a duty to repair your property as soon as possible once you find a problem and remember to provide your tenants with notice before entering the property. Most states and municipalities have laws regarding requirements for basic habitability, including heat, water, and electricity. The rental property also needs to be clean, sanitary and structurally sound.

As a landlord, you may run into a situation where your property requires extensive repair. For example, my rental property had a problem with the bathtub in the main bathroom. The bathtub needed repair and this bathroom had the only tub or shower in the house. The following was our action plan. We first had a reputable contractor look at the situation and provide us with a cost estimate. In the estimate, the contractor included a timeline of how long the work would take so we could plan for the work in advance and let the tenants know the schedule.

The work was scheduled to last a week, and since the tenants would be without a bathtub or shower for the week, we booked a hotel room for them for that week's time. The tenants decided to stay with family for two of the five nights, so we saved two nights on the hotel. Because of how the situation was handled, we avoided a major problem, got the repairs done in a timely manner, and provided the tenants with a place to stay that felt a bit like a mini-vacation for them. It was a perfect situation. How do you plan to create a similar perfect situation?

The first step is to create a plan and identify the extent of the problem. Hire a professional contractor to examine the problem. It is not a bad idea to get a second opinion. Have the contractor provide you with a rough budget for pricing as well as a timeline—you never know when you start a project what you will find when you start peeling away the surface. In our case, we did not know what might be found once the tub was removed. Luckily no hidden surprises lurked underneath that tub.

Our contractor prepared us with several possible scenarios, the timeline and cost involved with each. Another thing to consider is exploring if delaying the fix is a wise decision. Delaying may allow you to coordinate the project when the tenant is on vacation or even have the project completed during tenant turnover. However, it is vital to ensure that the property will still be safe if you elect to delay the project.

Remember to keep in mind a simple cost-benefit analysis of what you are working towards. Look at the necessary fix, the urgency, and if any additional improvements might make sense to do at the same time while the property is torn up anyway. For example, we decided while the tile guy was redoing the tile around the tub, we would also install a new tile floor in the bathroom for not much additional expense. That said, watch for scope creep to occur as a part of the project—scope creep is where you know the scope of the agreed-upon work, and then the amount of work continues to grow.

An example of scope creep is when you replace a light fixture in the bedroom and then realize that the rest of the light fixtures in the property do not match, so you decide to replace all of the light fixtures. Once you replace the light fixtures, the new lighting shows that the paint looks tired and needs to be freshened up. However, if you are going to do that, you might as well do new flooring, and it can go on and on! Discipline yourself to keep the work to what needs to be done and avoid scope creep.

Once you have the information regarding the extent of the problem, the next step is to speak with your tenants. You will need to work together to develop a plan for when and how the work should be scheduled. If the tenants are involved early on, it is easier to get their buy-in and cooperation. If the repair requires that the tenant spend time away from the property, see if the tenant has vacation plans or other plans for some time away when the work might be completed. If this is not possible, time in a hotel might be necessary. If they need to be away from the property, they might want to stay with family or friends. If this is possible, you should provide a thoughtful gift certificate for dinner out while they are staying with family or friends. They are saving you money by not costing you the hotel nights, and you should show your appreciation in some way. Prepare your tenants for the what if's and the things that might happen that will require extra time. Also, let them know what will happen if more time is required. In preparing everyone for the worst possible scenario, you will be under-promising and over-delivering when things do go as expected. You will also show that you are on top of things and prepared for the unexpected.

As a part of the plan, schedule a thorough cleaning after the work is complete and before the tenant returns home. Work and repairs are messy, and your tenant should return to a clean home along with the repairs being completed.

Thoughtful consideration of your tenants in this situation is important. Remember that while this is your property, it is your tenant's home. Keeping this in mind should help you develop a plan that allows you to complete the necessary work with minimal disruption to your tenants.

Once the work is done, remember to keep the receipts. Those receipts will come in handy at tax time. What other documents should you be keeping? The next chapter can answer that question for you.

Chapter 40

Keeping a Paper Trail

Running a business requires keeping records. Running a property management business as a landlord requires two types of records—tenant files and accounting records.

Tenant files include the documentation of activities, interactions and transactions regarding the tenant. Maintaining tenant files is imperative in the event that the tenant takes legal action against you or if you need to take legal action against the tenant.

The following information should be included in the tenant file

- Rental application, including information collected as a part of the application such as credit, employment, and references.
- Lease signed by both parties, as well as the rules and regulations sheet for your rental if you use one.
- Signed tenant inspection paperwork. If you took pictures, keep a digital record of those photos for future reference.
- Record of the security deposit; when it was received and deposited.
- Any bounced checks, including the date that payment was made after the bounced check.
- Repair requests and repairs made.
- Any complaints by or about the tenant.
- Any correspondence with the tenant, which may mean text messages, emails, or any other digital communications received by you, the landlord.

Accounting records also need to be maintained for your rental. These records show the expenses that are incurred to run the business, including supporting documents such as canceled checks, credit card statements, and receipts. These accounting records are for tax documentation. Keeping good records all year long will make tax times easier, and you will not be hunting around trying to find what you need before you file your taxes.

Many methods are available for maintaining accounting records—everything from ledger sheets to Microsoft Excel, Quicken, and other software packages designed specifically with landlords in mind. Software is only as good as the person that uses it.

Here is a list of accounting records to keep in the file

- Record of security deposit—both amount and date deposited
- Record the amount of the returned security deposit, and if the full amount is not returned, justify the funds withheld. Keep copies of receipts for amounts withheld from the security deposit.
- Record of all rent checks received
- Record the cost of all advertising
- Association dues, if applicable
- Cleaning services, including carpet cleaning
- Maintenance services and the cost of and dates of service
- Repairs, and the cost of and dates of service
- Insurance
- Legal and professional services
- Management fees
- Mortgage interest
- Painting and decorating
- Pest control
- Plumbing and electrical, including both the parts and service
- Supplies, including the software purchased to keep records
- Real estate taxes
- Utilities that the landlord is responsible for, including utilities paid for by the landlords when the property is vacant

Now may be a great time to interview and retain the services of a Certified Public Accountant (CPA) to prepare your taxes. Tax laws are more complicated for rental property owners. A CPA knows about the requirements for deductions and understands property depreciation that can be taken on your property. The services of a CPA can be worth the cost and can help you receive the maximum deductions possible.

How long should you keep records? The IRS recommends keeping tax-related documents for at least three years after filing taxes. Landlords should keep most other documents for seven years due to the possibility of litigation with former tenants and other possible business-related issues. Whether these records are kept digitally or in paper form is completely up to you.

Buying real estate is not only the best way, the quickest way, but the only way to become wealthy.

–Marshall Field

Chapter 41

Insurance

We touched on getting insurance as a part of the under-contract process, but let's go into insurance in a bit more detail. Insurance often seems expensive when you have to pay the premium. On the other hand, when you are paid on a claim, you realize the amount you paid in premiums may not have been that expensive. You are able to see the amount it would have cost you out of pocket to repair the damage if you had not had the insurance.

Now you are running a business, and someone else lives in your property. What types of insurance should you consider as a landlord? Did you know that homeowners insurance will not cover a dwelling that its owner does not occupy? Your rental property will require a different type of insurance. The type needed can depend on whether you are doing short- or long-term rentals. If you have decided to do short-term rentals like Airbnb or VRBO, you need a commercial-based policy. If you are doing long-term rentals, several types of insurance are needed. Make sure that you understand the insurance carrier's definition of short term. If you plan on sometimes offering a lease as short as three months, is that considered short term? Whatever you are doing, you want to make sure that the insurance you purchase will cover you in case of loss.

Below are the types of insurance you'll need

- Property insurance: Sometimes called landlord insurance, covers the structure, outbuildings, and any building contents you own at the property. It covers appliances, lawn mower, snow blower, and any other on-site equipment used for the purpose of renting out the property. This coverage protects you if the real estate suffers from a natural disaster, fire, earthquake, or irresponsible tenants.

- Liability coverage: Landlord liability insurance typically only provides coverage if the tenant or visitor is hurt in or on your rental property and you are found to be legally responsible. This policy may help you pay for resulting medical expenses and legal fees. If your tenant falls on the deck and the court can determine that the deck was not well maintained and had tripping hazards, you would be liable. Liability insurance covers the tenant's legal bills and medical expenses due to your negligence.
- Loss of rental income or rental default insurance. This insurance protects you from loss of rental income if your property becomes uninhabitable. For example, it applies in the case of severe mold or any other situation where the tenants could not live in the property. This coverage provides you with temporary rental reimbursement to cover the rent money you no longer receive if the tenants have to depart the property.

These are the three core coverages to have on your rental property. There are many additional coverages that you might consider that could save you some money in the long run.

A Helpful Hint! When purchasing property insurance, try to get a policy that offers replacement costs instead of the actual cash value.

Additional coverages can include
- Umbrella policy: This is personal liability insurance that will cover you in excess of other specific policies. This will protect your assets from unforeseen events and includes your personal assets in addition to your rental.
- Guaranteed income insurance: This covers the landlord if a tenant comes up short on the rent one month or does not pay at all.
- Vandalism insurance: This coverage pays if your property is vandalized. This type of damage is typically not covered by traditional landlord policies. Evaluate whether this is something that could occur, given the location of your property.
- Additional construction expenses insurance: If you repair a property after extensive damage, you could be legally required to upgrade the property to the current building code. This coverage covers the expenses incurred to bring the property to code.

Landlord insurance is generally more expensive than homeowners insurance because rental properties are believed to be more prone to damage. A general rule of thumb is to expect to pay anywhere from fifteen to twenty percent more than typical homeowners insurance rates. Check into bundling your insurance with your current primary residence and auto insurance for discounts.

If you have decided to rent out a home that you have used as your primary residence, you will have to obtain the insurance types listed above. Don't assume that your homeowner's policy will cover damages and liabilities while you are not living there. Contact your insurance agent to ensure that you get the best coverage given your situation and property. Also, remember that your insurance does not cover your tenants' belongings.

A Helpful Hint! Your landlord insurance will not cover your tenants' personal property. The tenant must purchase their own renters insurance.

Should you require your tenants to get renters insurance? This is a good question to consider. As a part of your lease, you could stipulate that the tenants must purchase renters insurance. This insurance will cover the tenants' personal property, which is not covered by your insurance. So, if, for instance, your property has a fire, your insurance will cover repairing the damage to the property but will not cover the tenants' property. A tenant without insurance will walk away very upset and could consider filing legal action against the landlord, as they seek to somehow be made whole. It is up to you, the landlord, to decide whether or not to require renter insurance. Some renters may be turned off by the extra monthly expense; others may not be concerned at all. Let your tenant know that renters' insurance can often be bundled with auto insurance to limit the cost.

If your tenant refuses to purchase insurance, consider having them sign a statement that says that you, the landlord, recommend that they purchase insurance and that they refuse. The statement should include a clause that says they understand the landlord's insurance policy does not cover their belongings, and if damage occurs to their belongings, the tenant is responsible. This clause, if added to the bottom of the lease, may help cover you, the landlord, if something happens. Please consult with an attorney in your area to make sure that this clause would remove your liability and to find out if you can require that your tenants purchase renters insurance. The bottom line is that good landlords educate their tenants, helping them make informed decisions. To protect you, have their decision in writing.

Chapter 42

Good Tenants Are Worth Their Weight in Gold

One of the most time-consuming parts of being a landlord is finding new tenants to fill a vacant rental property. You also have the cost of advertising, showings, and possibly no rental income coming in while you search for that great tenant. All of this helps you appreciate good tenants when you have the pleasure of doing business with them. I am referring to the tenants that take great care of the place, keeping it clean and the lawn green and mowed. These are the ones that treat the property like it was their home. What is the best way to hang on to the good tenants and avoid the tenant turnover as much as possible? Here are some tips.

One way to hang on to good tenants is to maintain the property and make regular improvements. A property with constant maintenance issues can be draining to both you and your tenant. It can take the pleasure out of living in a place for the tenant and can be costly for you as the landlord. It is important to take the tenants' maintenance concerns seriously and keep the lines of communication open. When tenants see that you are taking care of a place, they are more likely to do the same. Ask the tenant what improvements they might suggest or enjoy having as a part of the property. Take these suggestions to heart. They live in the place and know what it is like to live there. You may have never lived there. When you are improving the property and are taking the tenants' suggestions seriously, they feel like you care about their enjoyment of the property. You know that you are taking care of your investment. You may be thinking, "All of this costs money." So does finding a new tenant or the damage that a bad tenant can cause. You will also find that good tenants create far less wear and tear on the property.

If you have a great tenant in place, do you raise the rent when you come to the end of the lease? I have a pledge that when I have good tenants that are taking care of my investment, treating it like it is their home, I do not raise the rent for as long as they live there. My rental property is a business, and I know that I might be losing out on some additional income each month. However, I find peace of mind when an excellent tenant takes care of the property, and I do not have to worry about collecting the rent each month. To me, that is worth far more than the little bit of extra cash I would be collecting if I raised the rent. I consider it my gift to them and to myself. It is my way of letting them know that I appreciate them.

Having the right tenant from the start means that you have the best chance of a better tenant in the long run. How do you make sure that you find the right tenant? This goes back to thoroughly screening the tenant in the beginning. Ensuring that you have a person with the income to support the rent, creditworthiness, and a good rental history gives you the best chance of finding the best fit for your rental property. Taking the time to find the right fit can give you the best chance of finding that special tenant that you want to keep for the long haul.

Chapter 43

All is Not Always Rosy

The life of a landlord is taking the good with the bad and ensuring that you have plans in place to handle things that may not go as they should. Your lease should be your guide when tenants cause problems or do not do what is expected of them. These issues can range from a bounced check, late rent payment, no rent payment, noise complaints from neighbors, and unauthorized pets on the property. What you do in these situations depends on local and state law and your lease agreement with the tenant. These situations are never comfortable and can be difficult to deal with.

Imagine being in a conflict with your tenant. You want to resolve the conflict as quickly as possible with clear communication. I always feel it is in these times I earn my money. Rather than react, take time to read your lease agreement, make sure you know what is specifically expected of the tenant, and then develop an action plan for handling the situation. Keep emotions in check as you work through what you will do. Let's cover some of these common problems you could have and address how you might handle them.

One experience you may have as a landlord is an insufficient funds check from your tenant. How do you deal with this? Your lease will give you some direction and should spell out exactly what needs to happen. First, refer to your lease and determine how much you charge for late rent. When tenants write a check on the first of the month, and their bank account can't cover it, the rent is late. You have not yet received payment even though they attempted to pay you. In fact, they still have not paid the rent. You will need to let them know that the rent has not been paid. If it is in your lease, you may also have a charge for an insufficient funds check.

Armed with this information, it is time to call the tenant and inform them what has happened. Let them know the additional charges they'll need to pay. Here is an example of what I'd say in a phone call to a tenant.

> *"Hello, John. This is your landlord. I am calling because I received notification from my bank that the check you provided me with for this month's rent did not clear. Because of this, from here on out, I will require that you pay your rent with guaranteed funds. That can be a money order or a cashier's check. I will also need to have guaranteed funds brought to me today in the amount of the rent, plus the late fee, plus the insufficient funds check fee. That amount will be X. What time today should I expect you will provide me with that? If you are not able to make the payment today, know that an additional fee of X will be added for each day that the payment is not received. I am following the lease agreement that we both signed and agreed to."*

This information is delivered to the tenant very calmly and matter-of-factly. Notice in the example I said that they would have to make their payment with guaranteed funds. As the landlord, I would now require that the rent be paid with a money order or cashier's check for the rest of the lease period. Make sure that this is spelled out in your lease, so all parties understand this expectation. This policy will save you some stress and headaches, wondering if an insufficient funds check will happen again. If you decide to implement this policy, include these details clearly in your lease. Once implemented, you will no longer have to address this problem. If your tenant complains about having to provide guaranteed funds, remind them that this will save them money in the long run because they will not have to pay late fees or insufficient funds fees from their bank.

However, what do you do if the tenant tells you that they do not have the money? Ask them lots of questions so that you understand the situation as fully as you can. Make a plan with the tenant. The bottom line is you need to know when they will be able to pay the rent. If they have lost their job and do not have the prospect of another one, what is the plan? Do they have someone they could borrow money from to make this month's rent? Do they need to move out and break the lease because they can no longer afford it? Do not be afraid to ask tough questions. This is your livelihood, and you have a right to know. Yes, you are asking personal questions, but the intention of these questions is to get the information that will help you understand what is happening. It is in the tenant's best interest to be as upfront with you as possible and develop a plan so that they still have a place to live.

If the tenants are having temporary financial difficulties, it might be advantageous to structure a payment plan for them to follow. This could push the late fees and delinquent rent over the remaining lease period. The goal is to ensure that the tenant complies with the payment plan and that the unpaid rent and late fees are paid in full by the end of the lease. You could also negotiate a weekly payment option to aid a tenant with cash flow problems. A payment plan makes it possible for them to pay when they have the money rather than on the first of the month. This idea works best with tenants that are experiencing short-term financial problems. The hope is that by being flexible, you will be able to get your rent, and the tenant can remain in the rental.

What do you do when the rent is late? I do not like to have to charge my tenants' late fees. In my lease, rent is due on the first and is considered late after the third of the month. I will send a text message to tenants on the evening of the third to let them know that I have not received the rent, and if I receive payment today, no late fees will be charged. If they wait until tomorrow to provide the rent check, they will need to include the late fee — one day of the per-day late charge. Ninety-nine percent of the time, I get a quick response in return to this third-day message. Generally, the tenant has forgotten the date, and they thank me for the reminder. I then find the check at my office waiting for me when I arrive first thing the next morning. Sometimes they will ask me if there is somewhere else that I might like to receive it. I do not want my tenants to know where I live, so I ask them to drop it at my workplace, where there is a twenty-four-hour drop slot.

If you send the text and do not receive payment within twenty-four hours, call the tenant and ask when they expect to pay you and any other questions to get the information you need to know. If the tenant will not take your call and will not return your voicemail, send an email so that you have a paper trail in case you need it. This situation will require your involvement. Remember to remain calm and unemotional and provide factual information to resolve the situation.

If late payments are a recurring problem, it can be incredibly frustrating and emotionally and financially draining for you as the landlord. Strictly follow your lease regarding late rent payments. Follow up with tenants as many times as is necessary to collect the rent.

Another problem you may have to address is having an unapproved pet at the property. If you do not allow pets, then no pets are approved. What do you do when you drive by and see a cute cat sitting in the window or a dog in the backyard? The first thing to do is to contact the tenant. Let them know what you saw. You might want to prepare yourself for great stories like, "We are just watching it for a friend while they are on vacation," or "We just got it and were going to talk to you about it."

So you have heard their story, now what? No pets is a hard rule for me. That means *no pets ever*! If the tenant gets a pet, they have broken the lease. Now they have to decide if they want to continue to live in the property and get rid of the pet or move out. For me, it is as simple as that. You will need to be careful at this point. The tenant may agree to get rid of the pet and then not actually get rid of it. You are at a crossroads here. You have tenants that are not abiding by the lease. Do you want to keep them as tenants?

Part of being a landlord is making these difficult decisions. I know I may sound heartless and perhaps downright mean. However, I'm running a business; I am not the tenants' friend. I have a lease agreement with the tenant, and I expect them to follow the lease and do what we agreed to. They knew when they signed the lease that they could not have pets. I follow the lease; I expect them to do the same.

In addition to making contact by phone or text, you must provide notification of the violation in writing. The letter will need to notify the tenant that they are breaking the lease terms and that the animal must be removed from the property by a certain date. Also, inform the tenant if they do not re-home the pet, they face eviction. To keep complete records, your file needs to include documentation of what you saw and when. Keep track of all the details, and if possible, get a picture of the pet. Follow-up with the tenant to ensure that the pet has been removed. You will have to decide if eviction is the appropriate course of action if the pet has not been removed.

One of my early tenants were two young men; both of them were moving out of their parents' homes and renting for the first time. They were scared as I reviewed the lease with them. They then signed the lease. I remember telling them, "This document tells you exactly what I expect from you and what happens if you do not do what is expected. I follow it to the letter, so there will not be any surprises between us." They stayed in my condo for a year and moved on. Several years later, I bumped into one of the young men. He greeted me warmly and told me that I was the best landlord he had ever had, and thanked me again for renting to his buddy and him.

Situations like that tell me I am not mean; I am doing it right. Tenants like to know what to expect. Setting firm ground rules is the best way to let them know that rules matter and that there are consequences for late rent, pets on the property, damage, or anything else. You will have to decide if you follow your lease to the letter or fudge on things as you go along. I recommend the former.

Another problem you may run into as a landlord is a tenant that disrupts neighbors. Even the best tenant screening will not eliminate the potential for spats between neighbors regarding noise. Asking questions during the screening process about what the prospective tenants enjoy doing in their spare time may alert you to potential problems. For example, the prospective tenant that plays bass guitar in a rock band and regularly practices at home should cause you to reconsider this tenant, especially if your rental property is within a condo complex with adjoining walls. These noisy activities can routinely negatively impact the neighbors. If you choose to rent to this tenant, they legally have the right to play during reasonable hours. The property's municipality will have a noise ordinance; familiarize yourself with it. The neighbors may find the noise obnoxious, but the tenant has the right to engage in this activity. It can certainly cause friction between the tenant and the neighbors, who more than likely find the behavior disrespectful.

Often, the best approach is to allow the disputes to be worked out between the parties. You can help ensure that you are not involved at the first sign of a problem by having a clause in your lease that states that the tenant must make every effort to handle disputes between the parties without your intervention. The downside of this approach is that you may not know of the problem until you receive a phone call from the management company or police. At this point, your intervention is absolutely necessary. Your involvement at this point may require more than trying to mediate the situation between the parties and may instead require a more heavy-handed intervention like the "three strikes you're out" approach. This approach requires specific documentation that you can refer to later if needed. The three strikes you're out approach means that once you have received three verified and documented complaints, the tenant will be required to move out. You would have to notify the tenant in writing after each verified complaint. This may require eviction if the tenant does not leave voluntarily. To enforce this guideline, you must have verbiage in your lease that addresses noise complaints from neighbors. The three-strikes approach should be used as a last resort.

Lack of payments for utilities may be another situation that you have to address as a landlord. It is wise as a landlord to monitor your tenants' payments for utilities. Many utility providers allow the landlord to be signed up for notifications if the tenant is behind in payments or facing a utility shut-off. As the property owner, it may be possible to have the utilities switched into your name rather than having the utilities shut off. A shut-off due to lack of payment could cause damage to your property. The past due utility payment can be handled in much the same way as late rent. You can establish a payment plan and make it clear to the tenant that they are responsible for the past due balance. Whether the utilities are in your name or the tenant's name should be addressed in your lease and make sure that the lease is clear and specific regarding utility responsibility.

What happens if the situation does not resolve itself as easily as I have described? Mediation is a possible way to resolve any problem you have with a tenant. Mediation is a process through which a neutral third party helps the parties in conflict work out their differences. It is a voluntary process that will require all parties to participate. Depending on where you live, you may have low-cost or free mediation services available to you. Mediation is often effective in resolving landlord-tenant conflicts.

Another option for resolving conflicts is to make it easy for the tenants to leave voluntarily. As the landlord, you could say that the tenant is welcome to move, but they remain responsible for the rent until the property is re-rented. This might work quite well in the situation of the pet that is not allowed. You could agree to a timeline in which the tenant is comfortable moving out and you are comfortable letting them go. That might be thirty days, or that might be as soon as they are able to find another place, not to exceed thirty days. Put this agreement in writing so that all parties know what is expected of them. It is far better to have the tenant leave voluntarily than evict them. If the tenant will not leave and is breaking the lease terms, you have few options but proceed with the eviction procedures as soon as possible. You may *not* change the locks, forcibly remove the tenant's belongings, or shut off the utilities.

Conflict with tenants is stressful for a landlord. Let's look at tips for resolving conflict and de-escalating the situation.

Chapter 44

Tips on Resolving Conflict With Tenants

Disagreements with tenants can be a natural part of being a landlord. It is vital to resolve these disagreements quickly and effectively. Here are some tips on de-escalating the disagreements with tenants to resolve the conflict.

Tips for de-escalation:

- **Take immediate action:** The first step in working towards resolving a conflict is to take action. The conflict can often result from miscommunication or a simple misunderstanding and might be resolved with a simple conversation. Set up a time to meet with your tenant. It is ideal to meet in person, if at all possible and it is advisable to select a neutral location to discuss the issue. It is not a good idea to drop by your rental unannounced to talk as this can cause the tenant to feel awkward and possibly threatened. Your second option is a phone conversation. Do this only if talking in person is not possible.
- **Focus on the issue:** Stick to the facts when presenting information. Focus on the problem, not the person. Avoid any personal attacks. Be courteous. Make sure that problem solving is the goal of the discussion.
- **Remain positive:** Keep a positive attitude and a positive tone to the discussion. Keeping control of your emotions can help you keep the conversation calm and productive.
- **Actively listen:** Maintain eye contact with the tenant. Do not interrupt while the tenant is speaking. Listen attentively. After they have spoken, rephrase what they have said to make sure you understand what you

heard. By rephrasing what they have said, you are not agreeing. Instead, you are showing that they have been heard. Ask open-ended questions to get as much information as possible. Say things like, "Go on. I am listening. Tell me more. Is there anything else?"

- **Keep it simple:** Make sure that what you are saying is clear and easily understood.
- **Show you care:** Be empathetic to the tenant's side of the situation. Try to put yourself in their shoes. Seeing the situation from their point of view can reduce stubbornness and possible resentment.
- **Take responsibility:** If the conflict is due to a mistake that you have made, take responsibility for the mistake.
- **Problem-solving:** Encourage the tenant to provide possible solutions to the problem. Ask questions like, "How can we solve this, so it works for both of us? What would you do if you were in my position?"
- **End with a win-win:** Try to negotiate an agreement that will end with an option that benefits both parties. Show your tenants that you are compromising and making every effort to work with them. Doing this does not show that you are weak but instead shows that you are reasonable and making an effort. If possible, get buy-in from your tenant on the final solution. With buy-in, the tenant is more likely to cooperate. If this is not possible, make sure that your tenant still feels heard and does understand the reason for the decision.

A Helpful Hint! If emotions flare at any point during the meeting, take a time out. You can say something like, "Our best selves are not talking right now. I feel we need to take a break."

After the meeting, follow up in writing either by email or letter. In this correspondence, review the resolution. Doing this will ensure that the tenant understands. Sending a letter or email also provides you with documentation and a paper trail for your files.

If your tenants have broken the lease and you have asked them to move voluntarily and they have not, your next step may be eviction. It is important to know the steps to take. The process of eviction is not as simple as telling the tenant they must leave. The next chapter will explore the eviction process in detail.

Chapter 45

Eviction

Whether you have been a landlord for a long time or are just getting started, it is important to understand the eviction process and know that you may have to go through it at some point in your time as a landlord. Even if you are a good landlord and you have worked hard to build positive relationships with your tenants, at some point you may decide that despite your best efforts, the relationship between you and your tenants is simply not working, and it is necessary to begin the eviction process.

Just because the relationship has soured is not reason enough to evict a tenant. Legally, specific events must have occurred in order for you to begin the eviction process. The eviction process can be lengthy, expensive, and unpleasant for all involved. You will want to make sure that you have explored all other options. If you must evict a tenant, you will need to follow every step of the eviction process exactly.

What is eviction? A simple definition of eviction is the removal of a tenant from a rental property by a landlord. However, that definition does not speak to how serious an eviction is. An eviction has long-term effects on the tenant. It can affect a tenant's credit and their ability to rent another property in the future. It should be considered a last resort. When evicting a tenant, a landlord must follow the state and municipality rules and procedures. It is a legal process, and it is wise to consult an attorney before undertaking an eviction action. Though the process may differ from location to location, generally, it is the same.

The laws in your area may dictate otherwise, but in general, a landlord may initiate an eviction of the tenant for the following reasons.

Reasons for eviction

- If the tenant has failed to pay the rent.
- If the tenant has violated a term of the lease.
- If the tenant has committed a substantial violation which may include a violent or drug-related felony on or near the rental property, or has committed an act that endangers a person or the landlords' property.
- If the tenant refuses to leave the rental after the end of the lease. This includes a month-to-month tenant that has been given the required notice that the lease will not be renewed.

Notice that tenants who drive you crazy or that you simply do not get along with are not listed as reasons for eviction.

Laws differ based on location, but below are the general steps in the eviction process—ensure you follow your local laws. The eviction can be delayed or dismissed by the court if all of the details are not followed precisely. It is wise to have an attorney involved to avoid mistakes. Contact a local real estate attorney, preferably the attorney who assisted you with your lease, to assist you with the eviction.

Eviction steps:

- **Step one:** The tenant violates the lease.
- **Step two:** Demand for compliance notice. Once the notice has been served and the period of time outlined in the notice expires, you have the legal right to begin the eviction proceedings. In some locales, this process can be as quick as three days.

A Helpful Hint! Let's say the tenant owes you $1500 in rent and late fees, and you are pursuing the eviction because of the late rent. You serve notice, and once the notice is received, your tenant pays you the $1,500. The lease violation—nonpayment of rent—is cured, and you cannot evict your tenant at this time.

- **Step Three:** Initiate the eviction proceedings. If in step two you have demanded that the tenant pay the back rent and late fees of $1,500 and the tenant did not pay in the amount of time provided and did not move out, you may begin the eviction proceedings in court. In general, you will be required to submit a complaint to the court and pay a filing fee. The rules and procedures required by statute must be followed exactly. If they are not correctly followed, the court can deny the order. The court will issue a notice that both you and your tenant must appear in court on a specific date and time. The tenant will be served with the complaint and the summons to appear in court.

- **Step Four:** Once the tenant has received the summons and complaint, they may be required to respond to the complaint by a certain date. The tenant may offer a defense or concede that your complaint is valid. If the tenant chooses to offer a defense, the court will set a hearing date.
- **Step Five:** Attend the hearing. Both landlord and tenant will be required to appear in court. If the tenant does not appear in court, you will likely win your case by default. When you appear in court, be professional. Be prepared. Have your documents, including the lease and any notes, ready to present to the court. Present the facts as objectively as you can in order of occurrence. When the tenant speaks, do not interrupt. Take notes and ask for permission to respond when the tenant is finished speaking. In some parts of the country, mediators may be present to help the landlord and tenant reach an agreement before appearing before the judge. Any agreement reached with a mediator can become an order of the court.
- **Step Six:** The court will make a decision. Once the judge rules in your favor, you will receive an order giving you the right to evict the tenant. The tenant may be able to appeal the decision, and you may have to wait to evict until the appeal period has expired.
- **Step Seven:** Once you have the order to evict the tenant, it is wise to contact the sheriff to remove the tenant from the property. The sheriff will be required to provide the tenant with a minimum amount of time to leave the property.

An eviction is not a pleasant process for the tenant or the landlord. Conducting an eviction costs time, money, and resources. If everything goes exactly as it is supposed to, the process can take anywhere from fourteen to twenty-one days. If problems are encountered along the way, such as incorrectly filed paperwork or something as simple as a misspelled name, delays may arise, and the eviction process may take much longer. Some evictions take months. It is best to avoid eviction if at all possible.

Chapter 46

1031 Exchange—How to Sell and Wisely Buy Something Else

Let's look into the future. Ten years from now, you are a successful landlord. You enjoy owning your investments and being a landlord. You find yourself taking a serious look at your very first investment property, and you realize that it is time for some significant renovations on the property. As you think about it, you decide that rather than renovate, you would rather sell the property and buy something newer, upgraded, and updated. This is where a 1031 exchange comes into play. If you simply sell your current investment property and buy a newer one, you *will* owe capital gains at tax time. That could be as much as twenty percent on the appreciation and profits on the property since you owned it.

Please note this explanation is made by someone with a background in real estate; I am not a CPA or tax preparer. This explanation is an example and highlights what could happen. If you do a 1031 exchange when you sell the property, you will not owe capital gains taxes.

What is a 1031 exchange, and why is it important? A 1031 exchange allows you to avoid paying capital gains taxes when you sell an investment property and reinvest the proceeds from the sale into another property or properties of equal to or greater than value within certain time limits. The 1031 exchange allows you to defer the tax on the appreciation to a later date.

How does a 1031 exchange work, and what is the process? Below are the steps in the 1031 exchange process. To begin the process, the property that you currently own is listed for sale. We will call that property your relinquished property. You accept a contract to purchase and go through the process to sell your relinquished property just like you would if you were not doing a 1031. Here is what is different. Once the relinquished property is listed for sale, you contact an exchange company — ask your real estate agent for recommendations. The exchange company, for a fee, prepares documents that must be signed prior to and at closing. The closing occurs, and the exchange company takes the proceeds from relinquished property closing and then holds the proceeds from that sale until the closing on the replacement property you are investing in.

Please note: You will not receive the proceeds from the relinquished property at the time of closing. The exchange company will receive and hold the proceeds until you are ready to close on the replacement property. This is a key element of the 1031 exchange. You will walk away from closing the relinquished property with no money!

During the closing on the relinquished property, the buyer signs a document stating they participated in a 1031 exchange. Signing that document is the only requirement of the buyer. After closing on the relinquished property, you will then attend the closing of your newer, upgraded, updated replacement property. You attend that closing with your ID and a smile on your face. In advance of the closing, the exchange company wired the funds from the sale of your relinquished property to the title company. You sign the documents for closing on the newer, upgraded and updated replacement property and you are handed the keys. You have just participated in a 1031 exchange. It did not hurt, and you avoided the taxes you would have had to pay if you did not choose this option. This description is simplistic, but the process itself is not difficult. That said, specific rules must be followed to do a 1031 exchange properly; otherwise, you may end up paying tax penalties.

There are very specific rules that must be followed in the process of a 1031 Tax Exchange. Timing is essential, and the process may not be as simple as the example above. Real-life rarely is. However, the example offers you insight into the process. The replacement property purchased must be equal to or greater in value than the relinquished property sold. The replacement property could be several properties that total at least the value of the relinquished sold property. Let's say that the property you sold was a single-family home, and it sold for $400,000. The replacement property must be valued at at least $400,001. You could purchase a condo for $150,000 and a townhome for $250,001, or just one single-family home for $400,001. The property purchased to replace the relinquished property must also be used as an investment and be rented out. You cannot purchase a piece of land where you someday want to build a house, for that is not considered an investment property.

The 1031 exchange has other rules regarding timing. Sometimes you're not able to find a property to purchase before you sell the property that you owned. If this is the case, you are allowed up to forty-five days after the close of the relinquished property to identify the replacement property. If you plan to purchase multiple properties, you will need to provide a list of possible properties, as long as you close on one on the list, you are following the rules of the 1031 exchange. You have one hundred and eighty days from the date of closing of the relinquished property to close on the new replacement property.

A Helpful Hint! Please note that the two time periods run concurrently. The timeline starts when you close on your property.

This schedule gives you some time to find the right property in which to invest. Do not wait too long to find a suitable property for the exchange. Remember that the rules must be followed exactly. There is no grace period. If you do not meet the schedule, you will not be able to complete the 1031 exchange. If you fail to meet the exchange rules, you will have to pay the taxes.

This overview includes the major rules and the process for a 1031 exchange, but you'll also need to know other critical rules. A comprehensive discussion of the ins and outs of this type of real estate transaction is out of the scope of this book. This overview is intended to let you know that you can avoid paying capital gains taxes when you sell one investment property and purchase another. Make sure you work with knowledgeable professionals when contemplating a 1031 exchange so you can skillfully be walked through the process.

Chapter 47

The End—The Beginning

The inspiration for this book came from years of helping real estate clients become landlords. As I walked clients through the process from selecting properties to setting up their rental businesses, I came to realize that there is a vast amount of information that one should know in order to become successful as a landlord. Having a strong desire to ensure that my clients were successful, I answered many questions and provided helpful tips and tricks. I became aware that answering questions and providing them with tips still did not seem to provide enough information for my clients. I wanted to help them avoid pitfalls and have an enjoyable experience. This book fulfills my desire to offer a simple, detailed guide to developing a successful rental business.

Using this book as a guide, becoming a landlord is easy enough if you are willing to undertake the effort. You can do it. You can also use the book to look up specifics you may be wondering about or situations you're dealing with as a landlord. You need to know how much to charge in rent or what to do if your tenant wants to leave before the end of the lease. You can look these things up in the table of contents and see how I suggest that you deal with the situation. I addressed issues that I have had over the years of being a landlord and issues that my real estate clients have had. Please remember that there is no magic formula to success or any perfect way to handle your rental business. Through the book, I take a positive approach. The key to all of this is to get in and do it.

A good book changes your mind; a great book changes your actions.

–Derek Sivers

I hope after reading this book, you will take action. Through action, you change your life. Re-read the book, take notes, and highlight things that are important to you. Tell others about the book and discuss it with them. Decide if investing in rental property is for you and develop your group of trusted people to work with, including your real estate agent, attorney, and handyman, and get started. If you read this book and do nothing, you have missed the whole point of this book. Please take action and become a landlord—or make a well-informed decision about why you do not want to become one.

I strongly believe that purchasing a rental property is a great way to build wealth. As I have covered in the book, using your money as a down payment and leveraging can give you an amazing return. I feel that the effort involved is worth any headaches that one might experience along the way. In the end, I hope you feel empowered to begin your path to deeper financial security using the information in this book as your guide! Here's to the beginnings for you and your journey as a landlord.

About the Author

Lestel Meade is a landlord and a top-selling Realtor with Century 21 Elevated Real Estate in Fort Collins, Colorado. She is also a wife and mother. When not selling real estate, Lestel enjoys an active life in Colorado. She desires to inspire others to build wealth through investing in real estate.

Thank You

Thank you for reading this book.

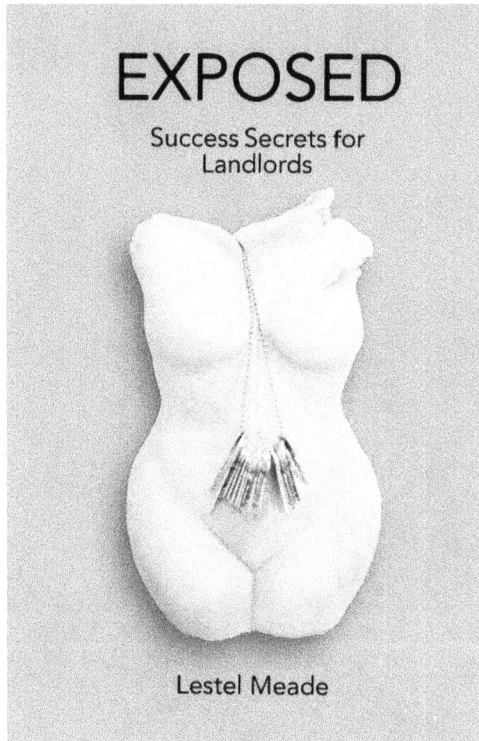

I would really appreciate your feedback.
Please take a couple of minutes and leave a review on Amazon.
I would love to know what you think.

www.LANDLORD-LAB.com/EXPOSED-REVIEW

Thank you so much and best of luck on your landlord journey.
-Lestel Meade